The Indomitable
Captain Matthew Flinders,
Royal Navy

Toussaint Antoine de Chazal de Chamerel,
Mauritius, 1770-1822

Portrait of Captain Matthew Flinders,
RN, 1774-1814
1806-07, Mauritius oil on canvas
64.5 x 50.0 cm

Gift of David Roche in memory of his father, J.D.K. Roche; and the South Australian
Government 2000
Art Gallery of South Australia, Adelaide

THE INDOMITABLE CAPTAIN MATTHEW FLINDERS, ROYAL NAVY

by Peter Ashley, MA

Lieutenant-Commander, Royal Navy

Pierhead Press
Clanfield

First published in Great Britain in 2005 by Pierhead Press,
Clanfield, Hants., England
www.pierheadpress.com

British Cataloguing in Publication Data.
A catalogue record for this book is available from the British Library

ISBN 0-9550817-0-X

Designed in Great Britain by Pierhead Press
Printed in Great Britain by MPG Books Ltd.

Abstract

Driven, ambitious, sometimes arrogant and occasionally reckless, few navigators had a greater share of misfortune than Captain Matthew Flinders yet achieved so much. This book is an examination of three periods in his short life, which serve to demonstrate his courtship with failure and his indomitable spirit in dealing with it. Firstly, there was his time in the *Providence* under Bligh in which he learnt the required skills of a navigator and astronomer, and was also where he contracted the venereal disease which would later prove to be the cause of his early and painful death due to kidney disease. Secondly, as commander of the sloop *Investigator* in which he circumnavigated Australia, but failed to complete the hydrographic mission ordered by the Admiralty due to the unseaworthiness of the ship. Finally his confrontation with his nemesis, General Decaen, on the Ile de France, brought about as much by his own arrogance and pride as by the hostile intransigence of the French anglophobe Governor which caused him to be detained on the island for six and a half years. The book is a brief examination of a complex individual, who contrived to carve out his own unhappy destiny and eventual premature demise before achieving the recognition he undoubtedly deserved from the maritime scientific community.

Contents

Figures and Illustrations

The author and publishers wish to thank the institutions and individuals for the use of charts, maps, sketches, paintings and portraits listed above that illustrate this book.

Glossary of Terms

able seaman   seaman promoted from ordinary seaman or 'landsman', the lowest adult rank

anchors   bower, the biggest anchors; stream, the next largest anchors; kedge, smaller anchors for special purposes, usually stored below decks.

bends   name applied to the thickest planks on the side of a wooden ship from the waterline or the turn of the bilge upwards.

best bower anchor   the starboard of the two anchors carried at the bow of the ship. That on the port side was known as the smaller bower, even though the two were identical in weight.

bilge   the curved part of a ship's hull immediately above the keel.

boatswain or bosun   warrant or non-commissioned officer responsible for the maintenance of the ship's rigging, anchors and cables.

brig   a two-masted square-rigged ship.

cartel   a commissioned ship sailing under a flag of truce in time of war to exchange prisoners or to carry a proposal from one enemy to another.

caulking   the operation of driving, with a caulking iron, oakum or rope junk into the seams of a ship's wooden deck or sides in order to render them impervious to water.

chronometer   timepiece or clock invented by John Harrison, used to calculate a ship's longitude.

collier   a ship built to carry coal.

commander	next rank above lieutenant in the Royal Navy prior to the introduction of the rank of lieutenant-commander in the early twentieth century.
cutter	a boat belonging to a ship of war, shorter and in proportion broader than a barge or pinnace, that is fitted for rowing and sailing.
draught	the depth of water required to float a vessel
flag rank, flag officer	an officer of admiral's rank, an admiral
grog	a mixture of rum and water served to the ship's crew.
hydrography	the study of the ocean's surface waters, particularly for navigation.
lieutenant	lowest rank of commissioned officer in the Royal Navy, prior to the introduction of the rank of sub-lieutenant in the twentieth century.
longboat or launch	usually ten-oared boat but could step two masts and sails, used as a ship's general-purpose heavy work boat
make water	to leak water into the vessel
marines	seaborne contingent of soldiers.
master	the most senior non-commissioned officer, or warrant officer, in the Royal Navy at the time. Responsible for the navigation of a ship, subject to the command of its officers.
mate	assistant warrant officer to a senior warrant officer, hence bosun's mate, master's mate, et al.
mulct	a fine levied for an offence by a member of a ship's crew. Recorded in the ship's pay book. Also levied for treatment by the ship's surgeon for venereal disease.
oakum	old pieces of rope untwisted, picked into shreds, and tarred, for use in caulking ships' seams, stopping up leaks, and sometimes in dressing wounds.

parole   a promise given by one in captivity, as 'an officer and a gentleman' - usually to not attempt to escape or take up arms.

passport   a written document from a State ordering uninterrupted passage and support be given to the specified bearer - usually a scientific expedition from an enemy State - provided stipulated conditions were adhered to - typically that no trade, espionage, carrying of dispatches or act of war was engaged in.

pilot   an experienced seaman who is especially qualified with local knowledge to guide a ship into or out of port.

pinnace   usually six-oared boat - often called a barge - used by the officers or for official purposes. Could step two masts and sails.

post-captain   the next rank above commander in the Royal Navy of the day and a necessary rank in order to be given command of a frigate or larger ship.

pox   all venereal disease was recorded as 'pox' in the eighteenth century navy.

sextant   instrument used to determine angular distances, usually of celestial bodies from the horizon, in order to calculate a ship's latitude and to assist in calculating longitude.

sappy   refers to timber which is still full of sap, green wood, not ideal for shipbuilding.

schooner   a fore-and-aft rigged vessel, originally with two masts but later with three or more. Designed for blockade running and as fast naval vessels.

shoot the sun   taking the altitude of the sun with a sextant.

sloop   originally, a term used generally for any relatively small ship-of-war that did not fit into other categories.

By the beginning of the nineteenth century, there were two distinctive classes of square-rigged sloops, the three-masted ship sloop (*Investigator*) and the two-masted brig sloop.

stem — the vertical timber at the bow of a ship that supports the bow planks

streak or strake — a ship's side plank.

wainy — refers to wood which is still green and thus pliant but not ideal for shipbuilding.

wales — extra pieces of wood bolted to the sides of a ship in positions where protection is needed.

Sources: Kemp, Peter, ed., The Oxford Companion to Ships and the Sea, (London, Oxford University Press, 1976); King, Dean, A Sea of Words, (New York, Henry Holt and Company, 2000)

Abbreviations

Adm	Admiralty Records
BL	British Library
FLI	Flinders Papers
HMS	His (or Her) Majesty's Ship
LCA	Lincolnshire County Archives
LTC	La Trobe Collection
ML	Mitchell Library
MM	The Mariner's Mirror
MS	Manuscript
MSS	Manuscripts
NMM	National Maritime Museum, Greenwich
NSW	New South Wales
PRO	Public Record Office, Kew
RANR	Royal Australian Navy Reserve
RN	Royal Navy
RNM	Royal Naval Museum, Portsmouth

A Note on Spelling and Terminology

The spelling, punctuation and grammar contained in quotes has been left unchanged from the original. The spelling of Flinders' father's name is correctly 'Mathew' with a single 't'. The use of naval language and nautical terms is explained in the Glossary of Terms.

Acknowledgements

Although my name appears on the title page, this book, while a record of my endeavour, would not have been possible without the tremendous support of very many people from Lincolnshire to New South Wales. My sincere thanks go out to every one of them for their advice, guidance and just for listening to me. If I have inadvertently omitted a single person I shall happily submit myself to six and a half years' incarceration on the island of Mauritius.

Perhaps first I should thank the Royal Navy who, while training me to become a weapon systems engineer, educated me in the ways of the sea and ships and ignited my interest in the history of naval matters. The research on which the study is based could never have been pursued without that thirst to explore where Matthew Flinders fitted into the 'age of Nelson'. Next, and of almost equal importance I have to thank my youngest daughter, Charlie, for introducing me to Matthew Flinders in the form of his statue outside of Melbourne Cathedral while she was spending a 'gap' year in the state capital of Victoria in 1998-99. That was the spark which set me on the road to becoming a 'Flindersphile'.

Next I must thank Lieutenant-Commander John Davies, from my time in HMS *Lowestoft*, who kindly supported my application to be admitted to the Masters degree course in Maritime Studies at the University of Portsmouth and to Chris Arkell for employing me in the Royal Naval Museum and allowing me four months leave of absence to further my research in Australia; also to Campbell McMurray, Museum director, Julian Thomas and the 'Friends' of the RNM who most generously awarded me a bursary which enabled me to attend the Baudin-Flinders bi-centenary conference on Mauritius in October 2003.

I visited a large number of museums, libraries, archives and historic sites during the course of my research and it is in these areas that I am fearful of forgetting someone, I met so many people, not one of them could have been more helpful.

In England I would like to thank the Dean of Lincoln Cathedral, the staff of Lincoln City Library and Michael Rogers of the Lincolnshire County Archives. Particular thanks go to Nigel Rigby at the National Maritime Museum, Greenwich, the staff of the Caird Library and Mary Edwards and Jerry Michell at the NMM Ship Plans division in the Woolwich Arsenal. Thanks go to the staff of the Public Record Office at Kew, and in particular to

Randolph Cock for his invaluable help with the 'copper-sheathing' of sailing ships, and to the staff of the British Library in London.

Among other individuals I must thank John Cawthen of Bromsgrove in Worcestershire, a direct descendant of Mary (Polly Flinders), one of Matthew Flinders' aunts, who has been an enormous help with the Flinders family history. Also Lady Marion Body, wife of Sir Richard, at one time Member of Parliament for Boston in Lincolnshire, in which constituency Flinders birthplace, Donington lies. Her kindness in sharing her knowledge of Flinders from the book she is writing about him and her hospitality at Jewell's Farm will long be remembered.

I am indebted to Professor Vinesh Hookoomsing and Professor Serge Rivière of the University of Mauritius for inviting me to attend and read a paper on the subject of Flinders' ship the *Investigator* at the Baudin-Flinders bi-centenary conference in October 2003. Particularly I would like to thank the Ly-Tio-Fane sisters, Madeleine and Huguette, of Mauritius, who kindly presented me with signed copies of their books. Also the thirty to forty Baudin-Flinders devotees I met there who made me realise I had joined a unique club and welcomed me to it. Apologies for not listing you all, but some are mentioned elsewhere.

Next to Australia: First to the Western Australia Maritime Museum where I was welcomed by Matt McCarthy, Sally May and Bill Leonard and given the freedom of the museum and its facilities, many thanks. In Sydney my thanks go to Lindsey Shaw, senior curator at the National Maritime Museum, and to Paul Brunton, manuscript curator at the Mitchell Library.

In Adelaide I discovered my second home and cannot begin to thank enough the people who made it so, and who have become good friends: Tony Brown, author of Ill-Starred Captains, who took me to all the historic sights, including Kangaroo Island where I was introduced to the hospitality of Mike and Cherry Hobbs in Penneshaw and Gabriel and Jacqueline Bittar at American River; Robert Sexton who wrote 'H.M.Sloop *Investigator*' for The Mariner's Mirror back in 1970 but who is as enthusiastic as ever about the subject; Stephen Milazzo the medical consultant who studied Flinders' journal and established the cause of his kidney disease, and knew all the best places to eat in Adelaide; Garth Morgan, the defence scientist (Oceanography) and RANR officer who had made an in depth study of the seas that Flinders sailed for the purposes of defence intelligence, knew the vineyards of the Barrossa Valley like the back of his hand and re-introduced me to Commander James Armstong from my murky past. What a day we had at Jacob's Creek; Tom and Anna Nelson, descended from a first cousin of the immortal hero. [Tom would have taken me to the moon and back in his old camper if I'd asked, great guy.] I am indebted to Rosie and Terry Schafer of Victor Harbor, overlooking Encounter Bay, who I first met in the RNM bookshop in 2002 and who made so many of the initial introductions. Also to Vivienne Causby, a retired librarian from the State Library of South Australia, who insisted in giving me one of her Flinders books from her personal collection. To everyone at Flinders University too many to name, except the three most important people of all, who made all this possible: Gillian Dooley, Senior Curator of the Flinders Special Collection, Dr. Peter Monteath, Head of History and the jewel in the crown, Sheryl Chandler, Head of Alumni & Community Relations. Sheryl had been the driving force behind 'Encounter 2002' and her dynamism ensured my three-month research fellowship at Flinders was a total success.

Finally, my appreciation to the three long-suffering lecturers in Maritime Studies at the Institute of Maritime Studies of the University of Portsmouth, Drs Ray Riley, Ann Coats and most especially James Thomas. No postgraduate student could have a more skilful, loyal and patient tutor. Last of all, but not least, my eldest daughter, Kate, for her desktop publishing skills, my wife, Lynda, for her patience and close friends for their support and endurance.

*Author beside statue of Matthew Flinders outside Melbourne Cathedral
(photograph by Charlie Ashley, December 2003)*

Preface

One day in early January 1999 whilst walking with my youngest daughter I almost literally stumbled over the imposing statue of Matthew Flinders outside Melbourne Cathedral. Despite my naval background and a life-long interest in the maritime history of Britain I was embarrassed to admit that I had not heard of this remarkable man before. In my defence I was, and remain confident, that I was not alone in my ignorance amongst the general population of the United Kingdom. Educated in the 1950s I was familiar with Drake, Cook, Bligh and naturally the great man himself, Nelson. I couldn't recall, unless, in all probability, I was guilty of day-dreaming in class of distant shores, being taught much about Dampier or Bass or even of hearing names like Banks, Baudin, Flinders or the sloop Investigator.

On returning to England I found a book by James D. Mack, Matthew Flinders: 1774-1814, (1966) in Gosport Library, although I soon came to realise that books about him are generally difficult to find in Britain. Once read I was 'hooked' and astonished at how much this little-known naval officer from the Lincolnshire fens had crammed into his relatively short life and I went in search of more and more information about him. Practically a national hero in Australia, his writings contributed to have the name 'Australia' adopted in place of Terra Australis. More than a hundred other locations around the continent are named after him not least of which is Flinders University to the south of the city of Adelaide overlooking the Gulf St.Vincent, first charted and named by him in 1802. His charts of the Australian coastline were so detailed and accurate that many remained in regular use until the middle of the twentieth century when aerial survey work began to replace them. He is also commemorated on the island of Mauritius where he was detained by the French between 1803 and 1810 and a bi-centenary conference for him and the French navigator Nicolas Baudin was held there, to which I was invited, in October 2003.

He sailed with Bligh and Bass from the South Seas to the Caribbean, fought with distinction against the French at the battle of 'the Glorious First of June' when serving in the *Bellerophon* while his work on magnetism is still remembered in every vessel that puts to sea with a magnetic compass today in the form of the 'flinders bar'.

I soon discovered that a great deal has been written about him. He himself was an avid journal keeper and letter writer and, thankfully, a wealth of original material exists primarily at the National Maritime Museum, Greenwich, the Public Record Office, Kew, the Mitchell Library in Sydney and at Flinders University in Adelaide, where I was given a research fellowship to study Matthew Flinders in 2003-2004. Without the scholarly works of the likes of Scott, Mack, Ingleton, Ly-Tio-Fane Pineo, Flannery and Brown and the support of Peter Monteath and Sheryl Chandler at Flinders, my research would have been much more difficult. This book in no way attempts to emulate the experts but instead seeks to examine afresh the character and personal ambitions of Flinders and the difficulties he encountered and the reasons why he did or did not succeed. While he may at times have been 'his own worst enemy', I cannot agree with Sidney Baker's description of him as 'my own destroyer', a phrase borrowed from Defoe's Robinson Crusoe.

Although it was his skill, humanity and courage as a navigator that delivered those who would follow him from the dangers of unknown coastlines, cannibals ashore, shipboard sickness, leaky ships and intransigent officials he was as much a political pawn in the maritime world of two hundred years ago as a corporate executive, or naval officer, of today. He was a fascinating study of human tenacity and frailty. Both remain relevant today.

Peter Ashley
April 2005

Prosopography - Matthew Flinders

1. Born: Donington, Lincolnshire. 16 March 1774

2. Died: London, 19 July 1814

3. Places and dates of residence and property residence:
    Flinders had no home of his own. On his return to London in 1810 he lodged in six houses:
    16 King Street, Soho, from 5 November 1810;
    7 Nassau Street, Soho, 19 January 1811;
    7 Mary Street, Brook Street, from 30 September 1811;
    45 Upper John Street, Fitzroy Square, 30 March 1813;
    7 Upper Fitzroy Street, from 28 May 1813;
    14 London Street, Fitzroy Square, from 28 February 1814.

4. Father: Mathew Flinders, surgeon-apothecary, died 1 May 1802
    Mother: Susannah Flinders (née Ward), died 23 March 1783
    Step Mother: Elizabeth Ellis (née Weekes), Married 2 December 1783, died 20 July 1841
    Daughter: Anne born 1 April 1812

5. Married: Ann Chappelle, at Spilsby in Lincolnshire, 17 April 1801

6. Career: Royal Navy Officer, placed on half pay as post-Captain, December 1810

7. Investments: Given 300 acres of land in NSW by the Governor, which he sold for £280 before his death. Interest on his legacy from his father and uncle gave him £120 per year. Funds from the sale of his investments in England, at his death, amounted to £3,498 16s 1d. Payment for his investments with Labauve and Desbassayns in Mauritius and Reunion continued into the 1830s.

8. Honours - nil.

9. Civil offices held - nil. Was often a guest of the Royal Society, before whom papers he wrote had been read, was not, however, ever elected a Fellow as Cook and Bligh were.

A note from Mrs Joanna Corden, Archivist to the Royal Society, dated 30 March 2004, read:

'Matthew Flinders was indeed never elected a Fellow, nor is there any lapsed election certificate for him. That doesn't necessarily mean he wasn't proposed, just that there is no surviving certificate. Unfortunately, there is no other way of checking, from our records at least, if he was ever proposed. (Since 1732 all Fellows had certificates citing why they should be Fellows, and although some lapsed certificates survive, they are few and far between). Lapsed certificates have only been kept on a formal basis since 1945.'

Pen Picture

In 1801, on taking command of the *Investigator*, Matthew Flinders was in height about five feet six inches; his figure was slight, but well proportioned with a light and buoyant step. Possessed of average strength he exuded extreme energy and activity. Of pale complexion his nose was rather aquiline his chin a little projecting and his lips compressed. He had a noble brow, hair almost black, eyes dark brown, bright, and with a commanding expression, amounting at times to sternness. His features expressed intelligence, animation and the ability to command.

*Statue of Matthew Flinders outside the Mitchell Library, Sydney
(Photograph by author, November 2003)*

Introduction

I have too much ambition to rest in the un-noticed middle order of mankind

Matthew Flinders, July 1804[1]

This book is an investigation, in three chapters, of a complex individual, Matthew Flinders (1774-1814) who contrived to carve out his own unhappy destiny and eventual premature demise before achieving the recognition he undoubtedly deserved from the maritime scientific community. It will demonstrate and contrast the 'highs' of his achievements in the field of maritime exploration with the 'lows', to which he sank due to human frailty.

He was not unique amongst great men in making the occasional mistake or indiscretion; but he made three significant errors of judgement, which were to change the course of his life irretrievably. This is primarily an examination, aimed at a better understanding, of three periods during his short life in which he unwittingly made those blunders and indiscretions but his indomitable spirit in overcoming the misfortunes which resulted; until the early indiscretion, his youthful philandering, finally brought about his early death.

Matthew Flinders was born in 1774 at the time of the American War of Independence, when Nelson was a midshipman in the *Seahorse* in the East Indies, Cook was on his second voyage to the Pacific and Bligh was still a midshipman in the *Ranger*. His short life spanned forty years filled with frenetic action, maritime discovery and writing; even when incarcerated on Mauritius he was never inactive. During this time the country was almost continuously at war with France as the two great powers vied for position on the world stage, and he died as Napoleon abdicated and England emerged supreme.

Flinders was the first to circumnavigate the continent of Australia and gave the nation we know today its name, although it was not recognised in his lifetime. Monuments commemorating his exploits exist in positions of prominence in Adelaide, Sydney and Melbourne, and in countless places around the coastline including a University overlooking Gulf St. Vincent near Adelaide. Beneath the acclaim, however, lies a complex individual, one who made his own destiny. Driven, ambitious, sometimes arrogant and occasionally reckless, few navigators had a greater share of misfortune yet achieved so much.

The first chapter looks at his time in the *Providence* under William Bligh in which he learnt the required skills of a navigator and astronomer but where, as a young midshipman, he foolishly but not uncommonly, contracted the venereal disease which would later prove to be the cause of his early and painful death due to kidney failure. Chapter two examines his time as commander of the sloop *Investigator* in which he circumnavigated Australia but failed to complete the hydrographic mission ordered by the Admiralty due to the ship's un-seaworthiness. In choosing to ignore or 'turn a blind eye' to the poor state of the ship's hull his remit to survey and chart the entire coast of Terra Australis had to be curtailed. Had the *Investigator* not leaked like a sieve from the beginning, Flinders' remarkable circumnavigation of Terra Australis Incognita[2] between 1802 and 1803 would almost certainly have been an even greater triumph of exploration and navigation. As it was, he did not complete the task ordered and thus did not attract the fame and admiration deserved during his remaining short life. It was only after the publication of his journal, in the very week of his death, that the world began to understand the significance of his achievements.

Whatever the reasons for the failure of his mission, the principal ones being inexperience, sickness, ill-conceived instructions from the Admiralty and his own impetuosity, none was as significant and debilitating as the poor state of repair and un-seaworthiness of the converted Armed Vessel, HMS *Investigator*, ex-*Xenophon*, when Flinders took command of her in January 1801. The aim of the second chapter is to bring the un-seaworthiness of the *Investigator* herself into clearer perspective.

This chapter will document the building record and assess the state of the ship when it emerged from survey and refit at Sheerness dockyard and explore the possible reasons for its poor condition and actions, or lack of them, taken to remedy the situation. It will examine continuing problems with the hull throughout the transit passage and voyage of discovery, which curtailed the task of charting the entire coast of Australia. This resulted in the ship's eventual condemnation and set in train the sequence of events leading to Flinders' incarceration on Mauritius.

Finally, in Chapter Three, his avoidable confrontation with his nemesis, General Decaen, at the Ile de France, and the causes of it are revealed. Brought about as much by his own arrogance and pride as by the hostile intransigence of the French anglophobe Governor, it was to cause him to be detained for far longer than he could have ever imagined. When calling into the Ile de France for nothing more than repairs and victuals, his pompous, if not abrasive, attitude towards Decaen, when even a modicum of tact and diplomacy would not have been amiss, led to him being detained for six and a half years.

When at last he returned to London he was a very sick, if not broken man. Too ill to return to sea and continue his unfinished work, he was placed on half pay as a post captain, while he spent his few remaining years in writing up his journals and charts which were only published the very week of his death.

Endnotes

[1] Flinders' letter to Banks from the Garden Prison, Maison Despeaux, on Ile de France, Historical Records of NSW, Vol.V, 1803-1805, p.397; Brown, Anthony J., *Ill-Starred Captains: Flinders and Baudin*, London, Chatham Publishing, 2001, p.389

[2] Greek astronomer, Claudius Ptolemy, in second century AD, was first to use name 'Terra Australis Incognita'.

Fig. 1.1
*Statue of Captain Bligh, the Rocks, Sydney
(photograph by author, November 2003)*

CHAPTER ONE

With Captain Bligh in the *Providence*

In March 1790 Lieutenant William Bligh had returned to England to face court-martial for the loss of his ship *Bounty* following the mutiny at Tahiti during the first breadfruit expedition. Later that year, on 22 October, he was honourably acquitted[1], promoted to post-captain and presented to the king while the first part of his account of his astonishing 3,600-mile voyage in an open boat from the mid-Pacific to Timor was published[2]. (Fig. 1.1)

Bligh is the connecting link between Cook and Matthew Flinders[3]. Cook was the first great scientific navigator, Bligh served under him, as Master, in the *Resolution* during the ill-fated third voyage to the Pacific where he learnt well the skills of scientific discovery. Flinders was about to become the heir apparent as Bligh would turn from being the pupil of the former to being teacher of the second. Notwithstanding the failure of the *Bounty* expedition, Sir Joseph Banks, President of the Royal Society and a staunch friend of Bligh, had persuaded the government of the economic benefits of transplanting breadfruit trees from the south Pacific to the West Indian islands. Thus it was that in March 1791 the Admiralty approved the equipping of a second enterprise for the purpose and a month later appointed Bligh in command of the *Providence* to undertake the task.

At that time Flinders was serving as a midshipman in the *Bellerophon* under the command of his patron Captain Thomas Pasley. Having become aware of the plans for Bligh's voyage Pasley recommended his protégé for a berth in the *Providence* for which he was accepted. Thus was set in motion the chain of events which would change Flinders' life, its course and length and the history of maritime scientific discovery inexorably. His father wrote:

> He is going with Capt. Bligh in the *Providence* to circumnavigate the Globe…and will be near 3 years performing this great under taking…God only knows what may be the event of such a long voyage may He prosper and befriend him in every Country, Climate and People…he has made much improvement in his knowledge of Navigation and is thanks be to God well and in good spirits…[4]

After a brief spell in the *Dictator* Flinders joined the twenty-eight gun, 406 ton burden[5], *Providence* on 8 May at Deptford Yard[6] on the Thames where she would spend several months being prepared for the voyage before moving

Fig 1.2
HMS Providence
(Ingleton, Geoffrey C., Matthew Flinders, Navigator and Chartmaker,
(Guildford, Genesis Pubs, 1986))

down river to Sheerness and finally to Spithead on 17 July[7]. (Fig. 1.2) With a complement of 200 that included twenty marines Bligh, ensured the security he had lacked in the *Bounty* was corrected, while his intentions to pursue further hydrographic work was evident from the substantial number of navigational and surveying instruments, existing charts and drawing aids embarked. Sir Joseph Banks was at the forefront in supporting the preparations for the primary purpose of the voyage and through his influence the two botanists, James Wiles and Christopher Smith[8], embarked to care for the breadfruit plant and any other specimens, which might be of interest to the Royal Gardens at Kew. Flinders quickly formed firm friendships with Smith and Wiles which would stand him in good stead in the future while demonstrating, even in his youth, the qualities of loyalty, principled behaviour and congeniality which would win him many good friends over the years. The expedition consisting of the *Providence* and the *Assistant*, a small two-masted brig, commanded by Lieutenant Nathaniel Portlock, to serve as tender finally sailed on 3 August. The first port of call was at Santa Cruz on the island of Tenerife where the ships remained for five days from 28 August. Here, perhaps for the first time, Flinders revealed his innate ability to record the detail of his travels and experiences when he wrote to both his father and to Thomas Pasley enclosing a small chart of the voyage thus far, sketches of the islands and coast and a description of the town and its people. He described the streets with balconied houses and the 'merry, good-natured people', as well as a visit to a nunnery:

> …we visited a nunnery of the order of St.Dominic. In the chapel … we perceived several fine young women at prayers. … None of the nuns would be prevailed upon to come near us … but presented us with a sweet candy … and some artificial flowers…[9]

This was indeed something new for an English country boy raised in the Anglican church of the fens.

The ships left Tenerife on 2 September but Bligh was so seriously ill they were forced to put into Porto Praya in the Cape Verde Islands for a brief visit before proceeding to cross the Equator on 3 October and set course for Cape Town. Flinders wrote an account of the 'crossing-the-line' ceremony, which he had to undergo, as it was his first occasion. His journal[10] shows Bligh fully recovered and in a benevolent light, allowing a degree of fun but not letting it get too rough and intervening when necessary to prevent the young midshipmen being exploited[11].

The ships dropped anchor in Table Bay on 6 November where they remained for seven weeks for repairs and to replenish their supplies of water, firewood

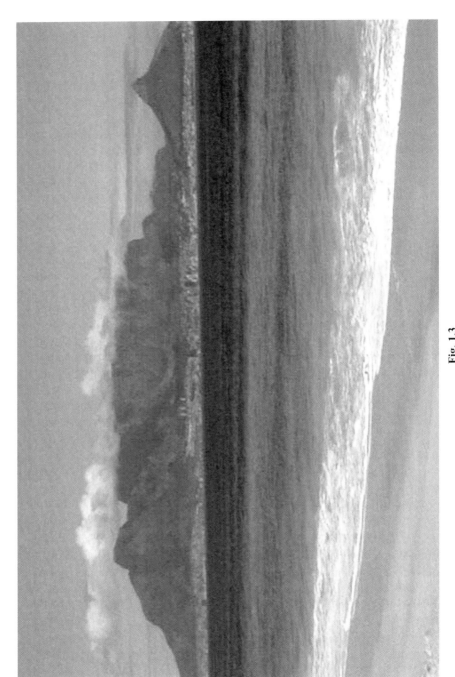

Fig. 1.3
Cape Town Bay
(photograph by author, February 2004)

and victuals[12]. (Fig. 1.3) Flinders once again wrote to both Pasley and his father with lengthy and detailed descriptions of the terrain and the people. He described the Dutch colonists:

> ...the Dutch, from having great quantities of animal food, are rather corpulent...they keep up their national characteristic for carefulness. Neither are they very polite. A stranger will be treated with a great deal of ceremony...of all the people I ever saw these are the most ceremonious. Every man is a soldier...they never pass each other without a formal bow[13].

The impression made on him by the formality of the Dutch stayed with him and may well have been responsible for his attitude and demeanour towards the French later in his life.

The voyage to Tahiti continued when the ships weighed anchor on 23 December and set course for Adventure Bay in Van Diemens land, now Tasmania, celebrating Christmas at sea with grog and sea-pie of mutton for everyone[14]. At sea Flinders learned the complexities of navigation, including the realities of trying to 'shoot the sun' holding a heavy brass sextant as the deck pitched and rolled under him and then attempting to correctly mark the ship's position on a chart. He became alert to the significance of the ship's sounds and movements and how to cope when things went wrong. He learned to watch the sea and sky for impending changes in the weather and possible hazards to the ship. His obsession for keeping records led him to copy the ship's Standing Orders, the instructions laid down to keep crew and ship healthy, clean and well-disciplined. He noted how the ship's log and other records such as the crew pay and muster books[15], victualling and armament muster books were kept and reported. After the ship left Adventure Bay on 24 February 1792 he kept a precise log of his own[16], briefly recording all the daily detail of a ship at sea: course, position, astronomical observations, weather, sail adjustments, cleaning, punishments, sightings and remarks, with small profile sketches of some islands[17]. It was in his journal that occasionally his sense of wonder was revealed as when he wrote one night, '...a blazing meteor...enlighten'd the whole Atmosphere'[18]. However, he was by no means 'star-struck' as was indicated by his recording of the issue of provisions, which agreed very closely with the account in Bligh's log[19].

The *Providence* and *Assistant* anchored in Matavai Bay, Tahiti, on 10 April 1792 where they remained until 20 July, in order to obtain healthy, thriving plants of the breadfruit and other fruit tree plants and shrubs[20]. (Fig. 1.4)

It was to be during this period that Flinders was to earn Bligh's criticism on two counts and for wholly different reasons. Little did either of them

Fig. 1.4
A view in Tahiti by Goerge Tobin
(Ingleton, Geoffrey C., Matthew Flinders, Navigator and Chartmaker, (Guildford, Genesis Pubs, 1986))

suspect that it was the second of the two which would dog Flinders for the remainder of his life, and eventually bring about his most painful illness and premature death before his achievements were fully recognised. Even after his death the root cause of his sickness was to go undiscovered for nearly two hundred years.

In the first case Flinders had been proud of the fact that Bligh had entrusted him with the care of the ship's three chronometers and had written to his father to tell him of his responsibility. His father wrote in his diary,

> ...with pleasure I note his being in favour with Capt. Bligh. He says he works observations for him, & that the Capt. Intrusts him with his Time Keepers[21].

This may, however, have been nothing more than a proud parent's interpretation of his son's general description of his duties onboard. Of the six midshipmen embarked, Flinders was one of the most junior. As his reliability became noticed it is quite likely that he was given the duty of winding the chronometers and recording their daily rates for comparison purposes, but it is more likely that this was done under the supervision of one of the senior midshipmen. In the same way as his flair for mathematics became recognised, he may well have been detailed to assist in the calculation of some of his captain's observations. Quite often three midshipmen were employed to read the time from the chronometers as Bligh made his observations; Flinders would almost certainly have been one of them. It was a Captain's duty to instruct his midshipmen and Bligh took this obligation very seriously[22].

On 15 May Bligh had set up his portable observatory at Point Venus in order to carry out daily observations, throughout June and July, in which to measure equal altitudes of the sun in order to establish the chronometers' errors and daily rates[23]. On 15 June an incident occurred which led Bligh to write:

> ...my young Pupils, in counting the time while I was observing over turned the Stand the Time Keepers were on - I could not have believed the accident would have produced such an effect, as the Box which contained the whole of them in their different cases, was prevented from falling to the ground or receiving, apparently, any violent shock[24].

As a direct result the Admiralty chronometer (Earnshaw 1503)[25] apparently never quite worked the same again, increasing its losing rate by 55 seconds. It appears that Flinders took the brunt of Bligh's tongue-lashing which was in keeping with his reputation for having a 'short-fuse' and resorting to strong language regardless of whoever was directly responsible for the accident[26]. Whether or not this incident coloured Bligh's attitude towards Flinders when he inexplicably demoted him to able seaman in April 1793[27,] and when he failed to recommend him for promotion, although he was not eligible to take the examination for lieutenant at that time, when the ship returned to Deptford in August 1793, has never been established. Yet when Flinders did take his examination much later, in January 1797, when serving in the *Reliance*, he was able to present to the board a certificate from Bligh that favourably described his 'diligence, sobriety and obedience to command' and his possession of the skills necessary for an officer[28]. However, the second and more serious incident arising from the ship's time in Tahiti is more likely to have coloured Bligh's opinion of the young Flinders.

Flinders' experiences during this voyage to the South Seas were to affect him markedly and in the final event fatally. It provided him with his first sighting of the then unknown continent of Australia, his first taste of the scientific discoveries in exotic new lands, and probably his first love. Tahitian women were a temptation that few eighteen year-old seamen were able to resist and the young Matthew, it is hardly surprising, was no exception[29]. Perhaps, though, he was alone in expressing an element of disappointment when he wrote in his journal:

> …their Colour which Cook calls a fine Brunette is no other than a tolerable dark Copper colour, certainly there are some of them may be call'd fair, but their Countenances are void of that Animation and languishing softness he speaks so much of…Constancy at Otaheite is not one of the Virtues…the Otaheiteans refine upon Nature in gratifying their Passion several Ways, some of which I should not credit was I not well assur'd of the truth[30].

His own words here are one of the rare pieces of evidence that he did indeed, notwithstanding any initial disappointment over their appearance, succumb to the languid and sultry charms of at least one Tahitian maid. Even as a young man Flinders was an avid recorder of all he saw and experienced on his travels but, perhaps not surprisingly, reveals very little of the inner man or any detail of his liaisons with women. Later in his life he was to write passionate love letters to his wife and, while incarcerated at Mauritius, forged good friendships with several of the French ladies. One in particular was very special, Delphine[31], the eldest daughter of Madame Arifat, but his private diary[32] for the period failed to reveal any possible depth of attachment in their relationship. Had he been a Samuel Pepys more might be known of his innermost self and intimacy with women.

Bligh, like Cook before him, was critical of the promiscuity of the native islanders and would most certainly not have partaken of the 'forbidden fruit' himself. Not only did he discourage the seamen from indulging themselves but forbade the presence of women onboard the ships. Before dropping anchor in Matavai Bay he had instructed the ship's surgeon to carry out an examination of every man onboard for any venereal disease in order to prevent its transmission to the native girls after arrival. Bligh recorded in his log[33] that five men had been found to be infected while Flinders noted in his log with approval that the examination would allow the ship's company to feel free from guilt in communicating the disease[34]. However, it was only a matter of a few weeks after landing that the prevalence of the disease became obvious, and, common and little understood as the infection was, the general attitude towards it was fairly blithe[35]. At the time of the *Providence*'s visit to Tahiti ships had been calling there for over twenty years and both syphilis and gonorrhoea were rife, the latter disease being perhaps more prevalent[36]. After eight months at sea the crews of both ships, including several of the officers and 'young gentlemen', 'chased after the native girls only to find that they were not chaste' - leaving many with 'warm tokens of their affection'[37]

Three weeks after the ships had arrived at Tahiti references to venereal infections appeared more or less on an almost daily basis in Bligh's log. One man was punished receiving twelve lashes for '...having connection with a woman while he was infected'[38]. The men were apparently undeterred though and the sick list soon climbed to twenty-two 'venereals'[39]. Bligh, suspecting that not all those infected were reporting their symptoms, once again, ordered the surgeon to inspect the whole ship's company. The boatswain and an unnamed midshipman were found to be among those concealing the infection. Whether or not this was Flinders, of six midshipmen onboard, leaves plenty of room for doubt but was immaterial in view of what was recorded later.

By the time the *Providence* sailed from Matavai Bay on 20 July more than a quarter of the crew were being treated for venereal complaints. During that period of time, the Admiralty considered such diseases the sole responsibility of the individual concerned. While officers apparently made private arrangements with the surgeon, all others, seamen, supernumeraries and petty officers, including midshipmen were mulct'd or debited fifteen shillings for subjecting themselves to the surgeons 'cure' for the disease. The mulct was debited against the individual in the ship's pay book and, at the end of the commission, when the ship paid off the mulcts would be handed in payment to the surgeon[40]. Flinders did not escape. The pay book of the *Providence*[41] has revealed that the young midshipman was mulct'd on two occasions for venereal disease treatments.

The system was unpopular with the ships' companies who would often hide their having contracted the disease to escape having to pay the surgeon for treatment, which was approximately the equivalent of two weeks' pay for someone of Flinders' rank. Then there was also the possibility of punishment being meted out from a captain with such strict views on the matter as Bligh. Accordingly the Admiralty discontinued the scheme of payment for treatment in 1795[42], adopting a more liberal attitude. Flinders would have been aware of the possibility of incurring his commander's displeasure and the effect it might have on his suitability for promotion in the future. For this reason it is quite plausible that he may have contracted the infection on more than two recorded occasions, which would probably have also gone untreated. The ship's pay book does not indicate where or when the two reported incidents occurred; but at least one was almost certainly while at Tahiti. The other could have been either at the Cape of Good Hope or even at Port Royal, Jamaica, the only other times when the ship made long stays in harbour and the crew were allowed ashore giving them access to women. Furthermore, the pay books do not record the type of infection for which the mulct was debited; the Navy of that period recorded all venereal diseases simply as 'the pox'[43]. That Flinders had contracted gonorrhoea did not become apparent until the nature of his subsequent chronic illness was understood.

The somewhat primitive level of treatment applied by the ship's surgeon usually entailed the application of a mercury-based salve or a solution of mercury nitrate used to cleanse the urinary passage, which evidently relieved the symptoms, although whether it was entirely efficacious was open to doubt[44]. No doubt the cleanliness of the surgeon's instruments used to explore and cleanse the passageway would also have been far from ideal by twentieth-century standards. This often led to the introduction of other non-sexually transmitted infections. In actual fact gonorrhoea is little more than a dose of influenza in the reproductive organ and the human body defence system will eradicate it naturally in due course, providing all sexual contact ceases and large quantities of non-alcoholic fluid are consumed[45]. In Flinders' case, regardless of whether or not there was further sexual activity, which was quite possible, dehydration brought about by the shortage of fresh drinking water further exacerbated the problem.

Although nothing in the nature of a mutiny occurred to mar the expedition, Flinders' journal did record that Bligh's harshness caused some discontent[46]. There was a shortage of water on the return passage from the Pacific islands to the Caribbean and as most of what was available was used to keep the breadfruit plants alive, their safe transport being the prime objective of the voyage, the men had to suffer. (Fig. 1.5) Bligh put each man on an allowance of a pint of drinking water per day 'exclusive of his grog', water use in soup and gruel was reduced by more than half[47]. Flinders was not alone, after all a large proportion of the crew had been infected with 'the pox', to lick the

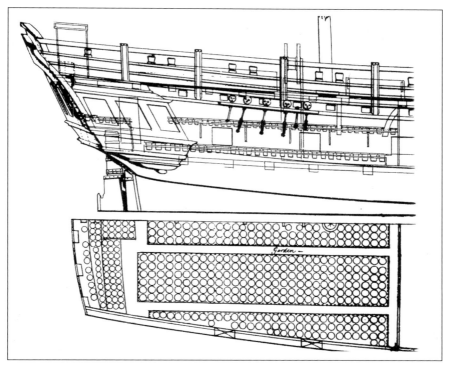

Fig. 1.5
Providence's profile and half-plan showing pot plant storage.
(Mitchell Library, Sydney)

drops of water that dripped from the cans and even from the leaves of the plants to assuage their thirst. Bligh would fly into a paroxysm of rage if he discovered a man taking as much as sip of water intended for the breadfruit[48].

From this time onwards, and for the remainder of his life, Flinders was to refer from time to time to his 'gravelly' feeling when passing water which would have been caused by crystals of ammonium magnesium phosphate in his bladder[49]. The mercurial treatment administered by Surgeon Harwood[50] in the *Providence* may well have introduced additional infective material via the urethra, causing more problems in the long term than did the original gonococcal disease. That infection would not have been present in an active or potentially transmissible form in later years, unless further infections from repeated venereal exposure had occurred, other than the two recorded cases reported by the ship's surgeon, and there was no evidence of this[51].

15

However, as Flinders was to demonstrate on more than one occasion, he could be his own worst enemy and in attempting to assess his own physiology in this case he made a life-threatening wrong diagnosis. No doubt his background as a surgeon's son enabled him to display more than ordinary anatomical precision in describing his symptoms and their location in the lower urinary tract, which led him to believe, according to his brother, Samuel[52], that he had a stone in his bladder[53]. His diagnosis, while erroneous, did not arise from any illogicality on his part and was entirely understandable[54]. It was, however, possible that recurrences of the ensuing problems would have been discussed with his close friend and surgeon, George Bass, when, while serving in the *Reliance*, he was based at Port Jackson for two years in the late 1790s. He was known to have been affected by scurvy on more than one occasion and the deficiency, when present, would most likely have lowered his resistance to infections and contributed to the severity of his 'gravelly' problem[55]. Furthermore, his incarceration at the Ile de France between 1803 and 1810 would have almost certainly have aggravated the situation. Péron wrote in his account of Baudin's expedition that the inhabitants of Mauritius were generally affected by:

> …all distempers of the urinary passages … to an extraordinary degree; they seem to proceed from the quality of the water which … contains a great proportion of carbonate of lime[56].

The illness, which would return again and again until finally it killed him, was still not correctly diagnosed; what remained certain was that it was a legacy of his travels.

The *Providence* arrived in Jamaica on 4 February 1793 when Bligh, in accordance with contemporary standard naval procedure at the end of voyages of exploration, collected the officers and midshipmen's journals for submission to the Admiralty. Flinders was unhappy with this:

> …as I had not another Book to proceed with, a Stop was put to my writing any more Account of the Voyage…[57]

When, six months later, the ship departed from the West Indies for England and the books were temporarily returned, he had to reconstruct his record from, '…Memory and the Ship's Log Book', adding critically, '…which I cannot say much for the Accuracy of…'[58] It had angered him not to be able to complete as precisely as he wished the account of his first long voyage, and demonstrates his attention to detail. Flinders was too disciplined to let his feelings show at the time, but was to write to Banks some thirteen years later airing his dislike of Bligh. He believed that his captain had been prejudiced against him and would rob him of any credit due for his work[59]. Not for the first time, and certainly not the last, Flinders carried a grievance over many years which was to prove to be without foundation when on 8 February 1812, Bligh, now a Rear Admiral, took Flinders to Buckingham Palace to meet the Duke of Clarence[60]. The future William IV was keen to see his charts.

Endnotes

[1]   Public Record Office, (PRO) Kew, Adm.13/102, Courts martial records.
[2]   Estensen, Miriam, *The Life of Matthew Flinders*, Crows Nest NSW 2065, Allen & Unwin, 2003, p.10
[3]   Scott, Ernest, *The Life of Matthew Flinders*, Sydney, Harper Collins, 2001 (1914) p.20
[4]   Lincoln City Archives, (LCA) Flinders, Mathew Senior, Diary and Account Book, 2/fol. 48v, entry of 20 May 1791
[5]   Bligh stated the tonnage as 420 tons, but the Admiralty draught plan gave it as 406 17/94 tons burden.
[6]   PRO. Adm. 106/3323 - Deptford Yard Book 1791
[7]   PRO Adm.55/152,153 Ship's Log- *Providence* (Bligh)
[8]   James Wiles later settled in Jamaica and Christopher (Paddy) Smith in Calcutta where he died young while Flinders was in Mauritius; Estensen, Miriam, *The Life of Matthew Flinders*, p.12
[9]   State Library of Victoria, La Trobe Collections (LTC), Flinders to Thomas Pasley September 1791, Flinders Papers, Manuscript Collection, 546/7
[10] PRO Adm.55 /97,98 Ship's Logs *Providence* (Flinders' Log)
[11] Darby, Madge, *Bligh's Disciple: Matthew Flinder's Journals of HMS Providence* (1791-93), M.M., vol.86, no.4, (2000) p.403.
[12] Ingleton, Geoffrey C., *Matthew Flinders, Navigator and Chartmaker*, (Guildford, Genesis Pubs., 1986), p.6.
[13] Flinders to Thomas Pasley October 1791, LTC, Flinders Papers, Manuscript Collection
[14] Ingleton, Geoffrey C., *Matthew Flinders, Navigator and Chartmaker*, p.6
[15] PRO Adm. 35/1361, Pay Books for *Providence*
[16] PRO Adm.55 /97,98 Ship's Logs - *Providence* (Flinders' Log)
[17] Estensen, Miriam, *The Life of Matthew Flinders*, p.15
[18] PRO Adm.55 /97,98 Ship's Logs - *Providence* (Flinders' Log)
[19] Darby, Madge, *loc.cit.*, p.405.
[20] Ingleton, Geoffrey C., *Matthew Flinders, Navigator and Chartmaker*, p.7
[21] LCA Flinders, Mathew, Senior, Diary and Account Book, 2/fol. 51v, entry of 29 January 1792
[22] Estensen, Miriam, *The Life of Matthew Flinders*, p.16

23   Ingleton, Geoffrey C., *Matthew Flinders, Navigator and Chartmaker*, p.9

24   Bligh, Captain William, *The Log of the Providence*1791-1793, (Guildford, Genesis Publications, 1976), p.158

25   Ingleton, Geoffrey C., *Matthew Flinders, Navigator and Chartmaker*, p.9

26   Tiley, Robert, *Australian Navigators*, (Sydney, Kangaroo Press, 2002), p.65

27   Flinders was restored to the rank of midshipman on 1 October 1793 after having rejoined the *Bellerophon* under the command of his patron, now Admiral, Thomas Pasley. NMM. MS. 60/017, FLI/5 - Flinders' Service papers

28   Flinders' certificate for lieutenancy, January 1797: Flinders' papers NMM, MS. 60/017, FLI/5

29   Flannery, Tim, ed.& intro., *Terra Australis:Matthew Flinders' Great Adventures in the Circumnavigation of Australia*, (Melbourne, Text Publishing, 2000), p.ix

30   PRO. Adm. 55 /97,98, Ship's Logs *Providence* (Flinders' Log); Darby, Madge, loc.cit., p.405.

31   Pineo, Huguette, Ly-Tio-Fane, *In the Grips of the Eagle: Matthew Flinders at Ile de France, 1803-1810*, (Mauritius, Mahatma Gandhi Institute), 1988, p.116

32   The Mitchell Library-State Library of New South Wales, Sydney, Flinders, Matthew, *Private Diary (Journal), Dec.17th 1803-July 4th* 1814.

33   PRO. Adm.55/152, 153 Ship's Log *Providence* (Bligh's Log); Estensen, Miriam, *The Life of Matthew Flinders*, p.17

34   PRO. Adm. 55 /97,98 Ship's Logs - *Providence* (Flinders' Log); Estensen, Miriam, *The Life of Matthew Flinders*, p.17

35   Estensen, Miriam, *The Life of Matthew Flinders*, p.17

36   Ingleton, Geoffrey C., *Matthew Flinders, Navigator and Chartmaker*, p.18, n.16

37   Brown, Anthony J., *Ill-Starred Captains: Flinders and Baudin*, (London, Chatham Publishing, 2001), p.39

38   Bligh, Captain William, *The Log of the Providence*1791-1793, (Guildford, Genesis Publications, 1976), p.168

39   Estensen, Miriam, *The Life of Matthew Flinders*, p.19

40   Ingleton, Geoffrey C., *Matthew Flinders, Navigator and Chartmaker*, p.18, n.15

41   PRO Adm. 35/1361, Pay Books for *Providence*

42   Ingleton, Geoffrey C., *Matthew Flinders, Navigator and Chartmaker*, p.9

43   Ibid, p.10

44   Flannery, Tim, ed.& intro., *Terra Australis:Matthew Flinders' Great Adventures in the Circumnavigation of Australia*, p.ix; Estensen, Miriam, *The Life of Matthew Flinders, p.19*

45   Discussion between author and Stephen Milazzo AO FRACP, Adelaide, 2 December 2003

46   PRO. Adm. 55 /97,98 Ship's Logs - *Providence* (Flinder's Log); Scott, Ernest, *The Life of Matthew Flinders*, p.24

47   Estensen, Miriam, *The Life of Matthew Flinders*, p.24

48   Scott, Ernest, *The Life of Matthew Flinders*, p.24

49   Discussion between author and Stephen Milazzo AO FRACP, Adelaide, 2 December 2003

50   Ingleton, Geoffrey C., *Matthew Flinders, Navigator and Chartmaker*, p.10

51 Milazzo, Stephen, AO FRACP, *Flinders' Last Illness: The Final Five Months of the Journal, February-July 1814: A Medical Interpretation* (forthcoming). p.2

52 *Victorian Geographical Journal*, Proceedings of the Royal Geographical Society of Australasia, Vol. XXVIII, (1910-1911), pp.11-30; Ingleton, Geoffrey C., *Matthew Flinders, Navigator and Chartmaker*, p.420

53 Tiley, Robert, *Australian Navigators*, p.210

54 Milazzo, Stephen, AO FRACP, *Flinders Last Illness: The Final Five Months of the Journal, February-July 1814: A Medical Interpretation* (forthcoming). p.1

55 Ibid, p.6

56 Peron, Francois, trans. Philips, Richard, *A Voyage to the Southern Hemisphere*, 1809, reprinted, (Melbourne, Marsh Walsh Publishing, 1975), p.47; Tiley, Robert, *Australian Navigators*, p.210

57 PRO. Adm. 55 /97,98 Ship's Logs - *Providence* (Flinders' Log); Estensen, Miriam, *The Life of Matthew Flinders*, p.25

58 Ibid

59 Flinders to Sir Joseph Banks, 28 July 1806: Mitchell Library, Sir Joseph Banks Papers, Section 13, Series 65.40.

60 Mack, James D., *Matthew Flinders*:1774-1814, (Melbourne, Nelson, 1966), p.230

Fig. 2.1
'Investigator' model: Port Adelaide Maritime Museum
(photograph by author, November 2003)

CHAPTER TWO

Commander of HM Sloop *Investigator*

The ship which would become famous, or infamous perhaps, as *HMS Investigator* was built at Monkwearmouthshore, County Durham by Henry Rudd and launched at Sunderland in 1795 as the *Fram*[1]. (Fig. 2.1) She was one of that breed known as 'Geordie-Brigs', sturdy little coal-ships or colliers built to withstand the buffeting seas up and down the east coast of England and none was copper-sheathed on build. She was built as a three-masted, square sterned ship with no head or gallery, with only one deck[2] and flat-bottomed of single three-inch plank with very stout scantling. Her dimensions were: 334 tons, 100 feet long and about 29 feet on the beam with a draught of approximately 14 feet and 19 feet depth of hold[3]. When purchased, or 'bought-in', by the Royal Navy at Deptford in April 1798 for £2,530[4], she was one of six[5] similar, but not identical, vessels initially registered as Armed Vessels, but subsequently re-registered as ship-rigged sloops[6]. The dockyard survey[7] recorded that the lower deck hull beams were 'wainy and sappy', an indication that the ship had been built using 'green' timber[8]. Given a major refit in the dock of Mr. Pitcher's yard at Limehouse[9] to render her suitable as an Armed Vessel and re-named *Xenophon*[10], she was weakened when large gun-ports of three feet square were cut in her sides[11]. Entered into the Navy on completion to carry eighteen to twenty 32-pounders on the upper deck and two 18-pound carronades each on the quarter deck and the forecastle, she was described as in 'good condition' and capable of 'taking the ground sufficiently well to continue using her guns'[12]. As an Armed Vessel she was complemented to carry a crew of 80-90 men and her dimensions were recorded as 100 feet 4 inches on the gun deck, 28 feet 5 inches breadth and 334 tons weight[13]. However, the Admiralty Progress Book did not record dimensions for 'keel for tonnage' or 'depth of hold', the former was calculated but the second estimated[14]. In addition, the work included the 'laying-on' of another deck to provide cabin accommodation. On build she had been rigged as a bark[15], but was refitted as a square-rigger overall. She sailed from Deptford on 6 August 1798[16], rated as a sloop[17], under the command of Commander George Sayer[18]. (Fig. 2.2)

During the following two-year period she worked with the Channel Fleet on convoy escort duties running out of the Nore and was seen in the Sheerness Yard for repairs during the summer of 1799[19], so she was not

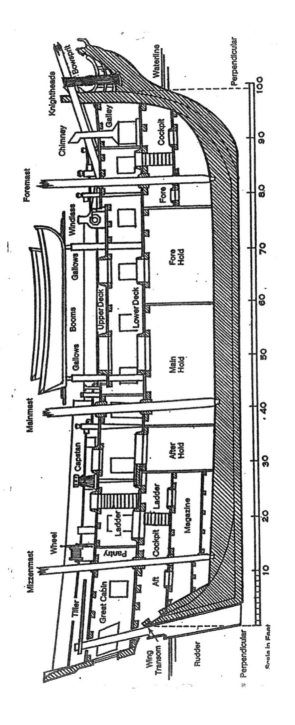

Fig. 2.2

HM Sloop Investigator - Longitudinal Section

(Ingleton, Geoffrey C., Matthew Flinders, Navigator and Chartmaker; (Guildford, Genesis Pubs, 1986))

unknown to the dockyard officers there before being taken in hand for the voyage to Terra Australis.

On 6 September 1800 Flinders wrote to Sir Joseph Banks from onboard HMS *Reliance* anchored at Spithead[20], having just returned from New South Wales, with his plan for a circumnavigation of Terra Australis. It was a bold move, revealing something more of the zealous character of Flinders. The letter itself was a *tour de force*. It drew upon almost every known argument, which would have found favour with Banks to the extent that some collusion on its form between the two of them, both men from Lincolnshire, was suspected[21]. Earl Spencer, First Lord of the Admiralty, was pressured by Banks and obtained royal sanction for the voyage[22].

In November 1800 the Navy Board wrote to Isaac Coffin the Resident Commissioner at Sheerness,

> ...we herewith transmit to you a state of the defects of his majesty's sloop *Xenophon*...and do hereby desire and direct you to cause the *Xenophon* to be taken on the ways at Sheerness, and her defects made good[23].

Mr. Whidbey, who had sailed as one of Vancouver's officers, was the Master Attendant at Sheerness Yard and knew exactly what was required of a ship to be sent on survey work; he gave much advice on stores and equipment[24], but there is some doubt as to the extent of his knowledge about the hull state requirements.

The ship arrived at Sheerness on 22 November with instructions for her to be taken on the 'ways'[25]... and her defects made good[26], this included the removal of her bilge pieces and instructions to copper her bottom[27]. She was docked on 3 December and re-launched on 13 December. The Progress Book[28] shows an original entry of 'copper taken off and re-copper'd', but that appeared to have been a clerk's error because 'copper taken off and re-' has been crossed out to leave 'copper'd'. So it was fairly certain that she had not been previously coppered and that was her first coppering. Although Flinders raised doubt when he wrote that on the advice of Isaac Coffin the ship was to be 'coppered two streaks [sic][29] higher than before'[30] to compensate for the additional stores to be carried. It was doubtful that she would have been coppered or sheathed in plank if she were engaged in the East Coast trade between London and the North East. Presumably, as she was built for the coal trade in northern waters and was not coppered, it is unlikely that she was copper fastened either. It is unclear whether the Sheerness Yard replaced all her iron bolts and fittings with copper ones when they coppered her. Had they not done this she would have run into problems with the effects of electrolytic corrosion although that should

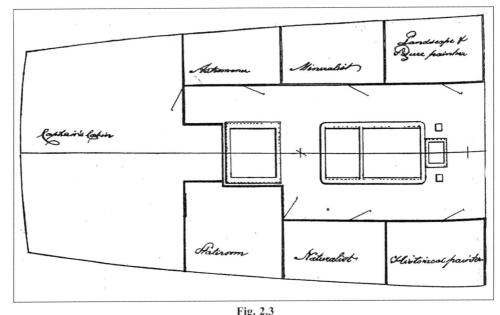

Fig. 2.3

Plan of cabins on Investigator's maindeck (later lower deck)
(NMM, Reg. No. 6224, Box 661, HMS Investigator Deck Plans, Sheerness Yard, 1801)

not have occurred for from three to seven years after. It would appear that she may have been coppered over already green, rotten or shipworm infested timbers. Although only five years since leaving the builders yard this could have been possible, there is no record of the state and quality of the timber used available, nor had a Sailing Qualities Report[31] been rendered for her since being taken over by the Navy. This would have been expected to be rendered by the commanding officer in the twelve months following the Deptford Yard refit in 1798. Flinders might also have been expected to submit a report in the twelve months following his taking command but by then he was heavily engaged in charting the south coast of Australia.

The letters and papers make reference to defects to be made good but there is very little evidence of detail of specific defects. There did appear to be an acute shortage of funds, in his letter of 22 November Commissioner Coffin reported insufficient funds to pay the ships' companies of nine ships at Sheerness[32]. It would appear that, apart from coppering, very little work was done on the hull of the ship.

24

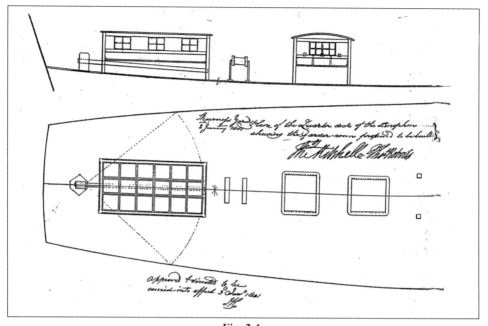

Fig. 2.4
Plan of plant cabin for Investigator's quarterdeck
(NMM, Reg. No. 6224, Box 661, HMS Investigator Deck Plans, Sheerness Yard, 1801)

That the *Xenophon* was chosen so quickly, and by whom is not known, indicated that some prior arrangements had been made. The standard procedure of nominating several vessels, together with preliminary correspondence between the Admiralty and Navy Board was circumvented[33]. On 9 December Commissioner Coffin wrote 'directing the dockyard officers to report the state of the *Xenophon* and the time it will take to fit her for foreign service'[34]. Five days later he wrote:

> ...to cause the defects of the *Xenophon* to be made good, and stored for foreign service, to fit her for reception of twelve 6-pounder guns, in the place of her present carronades, and for 2 additional cabins between decks[35].

It was suspected that the ship had various defects, which went largely unnoticed in the haste with which she was selected and refitted. Flinders, while ideally suited for a scientific voyage of discovery, lacked the experience of Cook or Bligh in dealing with the dockyard officers, and at that time had no Master to check the plethora of small detail necessary in preparing the ship.

It should be noted here that as he did not take command until 24 January, his degree of control over the refit work was limited. It was quite likely that the Sheerness Yard - allegedly notorious for their corruption[36] had skimped on the essential work of caulking and checking the timbers for signs of rot due to insufficient money for the project. Flinders was also distracted by his strong feelings for Ann Chappelle, their hasty marriage and her presence onboard before the ship finally sailed from Spithead[37].

On 17 December Coffin wrote, '...this morning his majesty's sloop Xenophon was put out of the little dock'[38] and the following day Flinders wrote to Ann from Soho, (note, he is not in Sheerness).

> ...a ship is fitting out for me to go out to NSW in. She is to be ready, it is said, in the beginning of Jan. ...Everything seems to bespeak the utmost haste, ... the ship carries 20 guns at present, and is called the *Xenophon*, but she is to be re-baptized the *Investigator*, and her guns reduced to twelve. It seems that promotion cannot accompany my appointment to the command of her; there are however some promises made on that head, to take place shortly[39].

On 21 December Coffin wrote requesting 'to receive sails for the *Xenophon* sloop from Deptford, Woolwich and Chatham'[40] and again on 28 December 'concerning the manner of fitting the apartments onboard the *Xenophon*'[41].

It was on 4 January 1801 Coffin wrote giving,

> ...approval of the drawing of the garden-room with the plan to fit it onboard the Investigator, the 2 cabins in the cockpit to be kept vacant[42].

The only extant plans of the ship which have survived are those of the gun and quarterdeck[43], made when the vessel was being prepared for the voyage of discovery. (Figs. 2.3 and 2.4)

On 22 January the 'order to call the *Xenophon* sloop the *Investigator*' (signed by John Moore in the absence of Commissioner Coffin)[44] was made and two days later Flinders assumed command of the *Investigator* when he wrote, the same day, to Banks expressing his pleasure with the ship while requesting his assistance in expediting the completion of the fitting out[45]. On 27 January Coffin wrote ordering,

> ... for the *Investigator* such stores as Captain Flinders may think necessary...and to make alterations in her cabin if they are of no moment, and to relieve her of such stores as may be deemed necessary[46].

and, on 5 February,

> ...the *Investigator* to be fitted for 12 long 6 pounder guns;...the clerk of the cheque to bear a complement of 83 men on her books[47].

On the same day Flinders was ordered by the Admiralty to complete storing with the utmost dispatch and proceed to the Nore to await further orders[48]. Coffin was still struggling to complete storing the ship, on 8 February he wrote,

> …Investigator to be provided with masts and spars from Deptford , Woolwich and Portsmouth…stores of the Investigator to be completed for foreign service[49].

The ship was finally reported ready for sea on 27 March and moved out to the Nore where she was delayed a further two months. Flinders used this time to make further changes to the armament and increase the stock of water carried[50]. On 6 April he wrote from the *Investigator* at the Nore, in which he asked Ann to accompany him in the ship which has space enough, '…with love to assist her, to be happy' but wished to keep it secret![51] Again on 13 April he wrote to her from Soho, in which he explained how busy he has been,

> …my greatest endeavours have been directed to getting everything ready for sailing myself, and in hurrying others;[52]

but he proposed a brief dash north to Lincolnshire to get married. The ship is only mentioned in the last line, 'the *Investigator* must sail by the 1 May if possible' His youthful exuberance and rash impetuosity were paramount; was his mind fully on the task and the state of the ship? His next significant blunder wasn't so much what he did but rather how he did it. He got married to Ann Chappelle in total secrecy on 17 April, not even telling his father. At that time, while not the general rule, it was not completely out of the ordinary for women to be taken to sea in His Majesty's ships although certainly no wives or family made the voyage to Australia on Navy ships without Admiralty permission[53]. Flinders did seem to have some misgivings though, as to how his plans might be received in high places, and had Ann discreetly installed onboard in the hope that he could get away to sea without her presence being noticed[54]. Sadly fate struck him another heavy blow, which would in due course alter his destiny. Earl St. Vincent, in the process of taking over as First Lord of the Admiralty from Earl Spencer, was passing in a boat as the *Investigator* lay at anchor off Sheerness and, being naturally curious about the planned voyage, decided to pay the rising young commander a surprise visit[55]. Of all naval crimes one of the worst occurred as no look-out reported the presence of the Admiral's launch; no berthing or 'side' party were present to greet him and there was no officer on the quarterdeck; it was clear that discipline was poor[56]. St. Vincent was thus able to enter the captain's cabin unannounced where he found Flinders with a lady in his arms! Explanation that she was Mrs Flinders did little to relieve the icy atmosphere

Fig. 2.5
Cape of Good Hope
(photograph by author, February 2004)

as she was evidently thoroughly at home being 'without her bonnet'[57]. Whether this phrase can be taken at face value, or alludes to a more intimate and embarrassing position ('*in flagrante delicto*'), has never been established. Flinders was certainly a passionate man as was revealed in his letters to Ann[58].

On 26 May the ship was ordered to proceed to Spithead, with Ann still onboard, only to run on the 'Roar', a sandbank northeast of Dungeness, allegedly unmarked on the chart supplied by the Admiralty[59]. A later re-survey of the area, however, confirmed that the sandbank's position had been correctly recorded[60]. Flinders successfully got the ship off without any apparent damage, after all, she was built as a collier and should have been able to ride minor groundings in the course of survey work. Whether or not she actually sustained any hull weakening damage was never revealed. In his report to the Admiralty Flinders made the statement, 'made no more water than she did before the circumstance happened'[61]. However, Banks was later to write advising Governor King in New South Wales, 'presence of wife on ship considered cause of mishap and lack of discipline'…he 'is not without enemies'[62] in high places. Flinders was most fortunate to have had the support of Banks and to have had Ann still onboard to take the blame for his being distracted or he may well have been relieved of his command. The ship arrived at Spithead on 2 June where she was delayed for another 6 weeks; Ann was put ashore.

On 30 June, *Investigator* was at Spithead, awaiting sailing orders, which were expected any day. Flinders wrote 'everybody onboard are well, and very anxious to sail'[63] On 7 July Flinders went ashore to the *Star and Garter* in Portsmouth looking for sailing orders to no avail[64]. The ship finally sailed on 18 July. It was not long after she got to sea that the many faults of the ship began to show. By far the worst and most uncomfortable feature proved to be the continuously leaky side planking. This major defect became apparent after only ten days out. On 31 July in calm weather a boat was lowered to examine closely the seams and butts on the ship's side. A heavy swell rolled the ship revealing the movement of the planks, but the leaks could not be located. Three days later, at anchor off Funchal, Madeira, the ship was heeled to port to ascertain the extent of the leak. It was recorded as taking in six and half inches of water an hour. The next few days were spent re-caulking the seams in the two 'streaks' [sic] above the copper sheathing but to little avail when the ship put to sea again on 7 August. The movement when at sea continued to affect her frame, the oakum worked free from the seams and water leaked in[65]. In the northeast trade winds the ship continued to leak at a rate of five inches an hour. Flinders wrote how he remembered that the dockyard officials had warned him of the ship's weak

Fig. 2.6
*Flinders-Baudin Commemorative Plaque over-looking Encounter Bay
(photograph by author, November 2003)*

condition and he wrote to Banks of the exigencies of the service being such that no better ship could be spared, but his anxiety to make the voyage precluded him refusing the vessel offered[66]. In fact, far from complaining to Banks he had expressed great delight with his command and its suitability for the voyage when he'd taken over in January.

At anchor in Simon's Bay, at the Cape of Good Hope, (Fig. 2.5) on 16 October, Flinders reported to the local flag officer, Vice-Admiral Sir Roger Curtis in HMS *Lancaster*, informing him of the serious leakiness of the *Investigator*. The admiral gave him every assistance, mobilising a gang of caulkers from the squadron to make the ship dry. For the next twelve days they caulked not only the ship's side, but every deck above and below as well while the carpenters painted ship[67]. While there Flinders wrote to Banks on 21 October, 'we are now under a thorough course of caulking which the leaky state of the ship in her upper works has made necessary'[68]. But when he wrote to the Secretary of the Admiralty, he made no mention of the leaking hull, giving only a brief description of the passage from Madeira to the Cape[69].

Fig. 2.7
*Detail of Commemorative Plaque
(photograph by author, November 2003)*

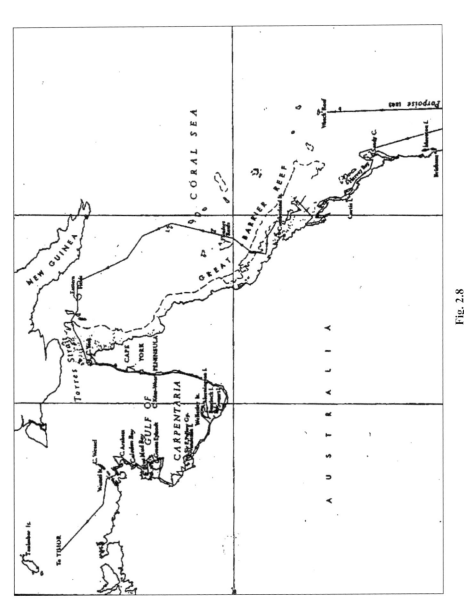

Fig. 2.8

The Strait and the Gulf of Carpentaria, 1802-03

(Mack, James D., *Matthew Flinders: 1774-1814*, (Melbourne, Nelson, 1966))

```
┌─────────────────────────────────────────────────┐
│                                                 │
│      TEN INCHES OF WATER PER HOUR               │
│                                                 │
│          HMS INVESTIGATOR's                     │
│                                                 │
│        APPROXIMATE HOLD DIMENSIONS              │
│             AT THE WATERLINE                    │
│                                                 │
│      80 x 25 Feet or 2,000 Square Feet          │
│                                                 │
│                  EQUALS                         │
│                                                 │
│     1700 Cubic Feet or 10,200 Gallons           │
│                                                 │
│                    or                           │
│           46 Tons of Water                      │
│                                                 │
└─────────────────────────────────────────────────┘
```

Fig. 2.9
Calculation demonstrating HMS Investigator's leakage
(author)

It was December 1801when the ship arrived off Cape Leeuwin, New Holland (at the most south-westerly point of Australia). New Year 1802 was celebrated at anchor in King George's Sound where the ship remained until 5 January. In his journal, Seaman Samuel Smith, wrote,

> ...at Night we stood on & off the Land, so as to be in with the Land the Next Morning[70].

A few days later Flinders noted that the rocky sea bottom was visible but did not record that the ship had touched bottom. Later it was found that some copper sheets had been loosened but this slight damage Flinders did not consider worthy of mention, regarding it as a normal hazard for a surveying ship working in uncharted waters[71]. It was, however, noted by Smith in his journal, he wrote,

> ...on leaving the Harbr our Ship rubb'd upon A Rock on one side & 14 Faths Water on the other; we afterwards Examined & found her Copper Loosened being the only damadge done[72].

By 3 February the ship was making three inches of water and this was to increase in the next few days as she plunged into a head swell causing some oakum in the seams to work free[73]. However, the leak appeared to be in the upper works so that by trimming the ship fore and aft the intake of water could be minimised[74]. On 22 February a different tragedy befell Flinders when he lost his Master, John Thistle, Midshipman William Taylor and six crewmen[75] in the cutter, which had been sent in to the shore. Despite an extensive search no trace was ever found of the men, although the remains of the cutter were found the following day. Flinders named the bay Memory Cove and eight nearby islands were named for the dead men. Later in March the ship's hull was once again refitted at Port Lincoln under the direction of the first lieutenant, Lieutenant Robert Fowler[76].

On 8 April the historic meeting took place between Flinders and his French counterpart in the *Géographe*, Nicolas Baudin, in Encounter Bay off the south Australian coast near the present day town of Victor Harbor. (Figs. 2.6 and 2.7) On 26 April, after the ship had grounded yet again (the third time since leaving the Nore) on a shoal off the present South Channel leading to Port Philip, Flinders wrote, 'no danger is to be feared from these banks [of mud] to a flat-floored ship'[77]. The extent, however, of unseen hull-weakening damage was not considered. Only two days later on 28 April the *Investigator* grounded once again on a mud bank in the sea area to the southeast of the present day Mornington Peninsula. Flinders wrote again in his journal dismissing the potential damaging effect on the vessel of these groundings[78].

On 9 May he reached Port Jackson via the Bass Strait and the scheduled refitting of the Investigator went forward as planned[79]. On 20 May Flinders wrote to Banks:

> ...I hope to be ready for sea again in two months after our arrival, victualled and refitted for 10 or 12 months[80]...the refitting of Investigator went forward; the portable greenhouse was erected on the poop[81].

At the same time he had the barricade around the quarterdeck cut down in height to facilitate the greater ease of taking of bearings from the binnacle. However, the construction of the deckhouse for the collection of plants would almost certainly have raised the centre of gravity of the vessel. This would have reduced the ship's sea-keeping qualities and caused her to roll more steeply and increase the ingress of water through the side planking.

After twelve weeks in port the *Investigator* sailed northwards from Port Jackson on 22 July in company with the brig *Lady Nelson*[82] to continue

Flinders' task of surveying and charting the coastal waters around the entire continent. Further groundings on sandbanks occurred on 27 August[83] and 8 September[84]. Minor incidents of grounding would not have been unexpected when surveying uncharted coastal waters, but the *Investigator*, while designed to operate in shallow water and even sit on the bottom, was in such a poor state of repair that it would preclude her being fit to complete the work. On 13 September she was caught on a bank of quick sand with the tide quickly sweeping her broadside on and making the ship heel alarmingly[85]. Only some adroit seamanship in quickly reducing sail saved the ship from being totally lost.

On 10 October Flinders wrote to the Governor of New South Wales, Philip Gidley King, from off the Cumberland Rocks [east coast of Queensland approximately 21 degrees south] reporting problems with the brig, *Lady Nelson*, his decision to order her back to Port Jackson with an abstract of the survey/chart work achieved thus far[86]. He made no mention at all of the state of the *Investigator*'s hull[87].

On 16 November in the Gulf of Carpentaria, (Fig. 2.8) it was noted that ever since passing through the Torres Strait, and as the ship made her way southwards and then northwards along the gulf's shores, a leak, which had festered long as a running sore, broke out into something more damaging. When the wind was on the beam, and the ship heeling over, up to ten inches of water per hour, but as much as twelve and sometimes fourteen, were reported by the carpenter[88]. (Fig. 2.9) During this period the ship had been generally heeling to starboard, which had led Flinders to suspect that the main leak was in the planking on the starboard bow. On 21 November the ship anchored off Sweers Islands and the carpenters began the urgent task of re-caulking. However, as they progressed they discovered an ever-increasing number of areas of rot in planks, 'wales'[89] or 'bends'[90], timbers and tree-nails, the list of parts affected by decay was deplorably long[91]. The ship was in an advanced state of decay. The master and the carpenter believed that if the ship met with a heavy gale and worked her timbers, or if she happened to get driven ashore in anything but calm weather, or even if an attempt was made to heave her down on her beam ends on a good beach, she would go to pieces. John Aken, the master, with his knowledge of ships of this type, judged she would last barely six months more'[92].

Flinders wrote in his record of the voyage,

> ...the ship having made ten inches of water an hour, in a common fresh breeze, we judge from that, and what we have now seen, ...that in a strong gale, with much sea running, the ship would hardly escape foundering[93].

35

Faced with this dire situation he had to contemplate the necessity to curtail his surveying programme and make an early return to Port Jackson. While he decided to complete the survey of the Gulf of Carpentaria, which was to take another four months, before running for Timor and then southwest and east about New Holland to Port Jackson, he was mortified by the need to terminate his work early[94]. The voyage was thus cut short in March 1803, near the Wessel Islands, due to the approach of the monsoon season and the stark realisation that the increased intake of water was being caused by the rapid deterioration of the vessel's fabric. His over-optimistic and high expectations for the complete fulfilment of his mission had been rudely shattered because of the rotten state of his 'copper-bottomed' ship.

Off the Island of Timor, on 28 March, Flinders wrote to Banks:

> ... in England and during the passage out I attributed the weak state of the ship to her large ports and the ill-putting together of her frame, but now it should appear to have arisen more from so large a proportion of the timbers being rotten. She made seven inches of water per hour soon after crossing the equator, but from lightening her upper works, and a thorough caulking at the Cape, she did not anymore admit so much during the passage to Port Jackson. For a few hours she made more than ten inches [of water] near the Prince of Wales Islands, [Torres Strait] and I had her caulked at the head of the gulph, [sic] on which occasion it was that the rotten state of the plank and timbers in every part of her was discovered ....to an observation of mine that the *Investigator* would not last out the voyage, I think, Sir Joseph, you once replied that the Admiralty must then send out another ship to me; but the dread of remaining idle for so long a period as until a ship might arrive from England deters me from thinking of it[95].

In the eighteen months after sailing from Spithead Flinders had never again mentioned the poor state of the ship to Ann in his letters until 28 March. From the *Investigator* off Timor, he wrote, 'the poor ship is worn out - she is decayed in both skin and bone'. He further wrote, ' the voyage is nearly half completed, and that we are all in good spirits and tolerable health'[96], thereby concealing the true extent of his own and the crew's poor health, probably not wishing to worry Ann.

During May the ship was again almost lost when at anchor near Goose Island in the Archipelago of the Recherche. Finding the ship drifting on shore where there was a tremendous surf running, and unable to weigh anchor, Flinders was forced to cut and run leaving both anchors and make sail[97]. (Fig. 2.10)

On 9 June he arrived back at Port Jackson via the west and south coasts of New Holland and wrote to Ann again on 25 June:

...a survey has been held up on her [*Investigator*] which proves her to be very much decayed as to be totally irreparable. It was the unanimous opinion of the surveying officers that had we met a severe gale of wind in the passage from Timor, that she must have been crushed like an egg and gone down. I was partly aware of her bad state and returned sooner to Port Jackson on that account, before the worst weather came[98].

He had not been at all well himself, nor many of the crew, and his cat Trim had turned grey. His greatest ambition to complete the directed task of surveying and charting the entire coastline of the continent, which at least he had proved to be one, was rudely shattered because of the rotten state of the hull of his 'copper-bottomed' ship - H M Sloop *Investigator*. (Fig. 2.11)

Why the sloop was in such a poor condition only five years after leaving the builder's yard remains unclear. Although built to a similar design as Cook's *Endeavour*, an acute shortage of oak during the late eighteenth century resulted in trials with softwoods, some fifty small ships were thus built, however they proved to be useless after a few years[99]. There is no record that the *Xenophon/Investigator* was one of them, although it seems likely in view of what transpired.

Remarkably the ship was refitted, modified and re-rigged as a brig at Port Jackson in 1804 and returned to England in October 1805. Her captain, William Kent, reported that a '...more deplorable crazy vessel than the *Investigator* is perhaps not to be seen'. Laid up as a hulk in Devonport until 1810 she was condemned by the Navy Board on 28 July but, instead of being broken up as had been assumed[100], she was sold by private contract to George Baily in December 1810 for £1,253. Under her original name of *Xenophon* she was extensively refitted and re-coppered and continued in the merchant service until broken up at Williamstown, near Melbourne in 1872[101].

Endnotes

1   Austin, K.A., *The Voyage of the Investigator: Commander Matthew Flinders RN*, Adelaide, Rigby (Seal Books) 1968 (1964) p.39.

2   Geeson, N.T., and Sexton, R.T., *H.M. Sloop Investigator*, The Mariners Mirror, Vol.56, (1970), p.277

3   Ibid.
    Public Record Office, Kew (PRO) ADM106/3412 - Deptford Yard letter dated 11 July

4   1798

5   The others were *Hermes, Selby, William, Ann* and *Albion*

6   PRO ADM180/23, f.90 & 113, Dimension Book

7   PRO ADM 106/3368, f.30, Deptford Yard Book, second series

8   Building Materials. Colledge J. J., revised by Warlow, Lt-Cdr Ben, *Ships of the Royal Navy*, London, Greenhill Books, 2003, p.11.

9   Geeson, N.T., and Sexton, R.T., *H.M. Sloop Investigator*, p.277

10 Austin, K.A., *The Voyage of the Investigator*, p.39

11 Ingleton, Geoffrey, C., *Matthew Flinders Navigator and Chartmaker*, Guildford, Genesis Pubs. 1986 p.429

12 PRO ADM106/3412 - Deptford Yard letter dated 17th April 1798

13 PRO ADM 180/23 f.90, 113 - Dimension Book

14 Ingleton, Geoffrey, C., *Matthew Flinders Navigator and Chartmaker*, p.428

15 Kemp, Peter, ed., *The Oxford Companion to Ships and the Sea*, London, Oxford University Press, 1976, p.60

16 PRO ADM 180/9, f.663, Progress Books

17 Kemp, Peter, ed., *The Oxford Companion to Ships and the Sea*, p.810

18 G.Sayer was not promoted Captain until 14 February 1801 after he'd relinquished command of the *Xenophon/Investigator*. Geeson, N.T., and Sexton, R.T., *H.M. Sloop Investigator*, p.278; Syrett, David and Dinardo R.L., *The Commissioned Sea Officers of the Royal Navy 1660-1815*, Aldershot, Scolar Press for Navy Records Society, 1994, p.396; O'Byrne, William R., *A Naval Biographical Dictionary*, 2 Vols., Polstead, Suffolk, J B Hayward and Son, 1990, Vol.II, p.1032.

19 PRO ADM 106/3555, Sheerness Yard Letters, 1798-1799

20 SL of NSW (State Library of New South Wales) - Mitchell Library: Sir Joseph Banks papers, Section 13, Series 65

21 Tiley, Robert, *Australian Navigators*, Sydney, Kangaroo Press, 2002 p.80

22 Ritchie, G.S., *The Admiralty Chart*, London, Hollis and Carter, 1967, p.69

23 PRO ADM 2/293/484, Navy Board Letter of 21 November 1800

24 Ritchie, G.S., *The Admiralty Chart*, p.70

25 Kemp, Peter, ed., *The Oxford Companion to Ships and the Sea*, p.929

26 PRO ADM 106/3556.50, Sheerness Yard Letters, 1800-1801

27 PRO ADM 106/3556.53, Sheerness Yard Letters, 1800-1801

28 PRO ADM 180/9, f.663, Progress Books

29 Kemp, Peter, ed., *The Oxford Companion to Ships and the Sea*, p.838

30 Flinders, Matthew, Capt. RN, *A Voyage to Terra Australis*, 2 Vols. Atlas, London, G & W Nicol, 1814, Vol. 1, p.4

Fig. 2.10
Best Bower anchor from HMS Investigator, recovered in 1973, Maritime Museum, Port Adelaide (photograph by author, November 2003)

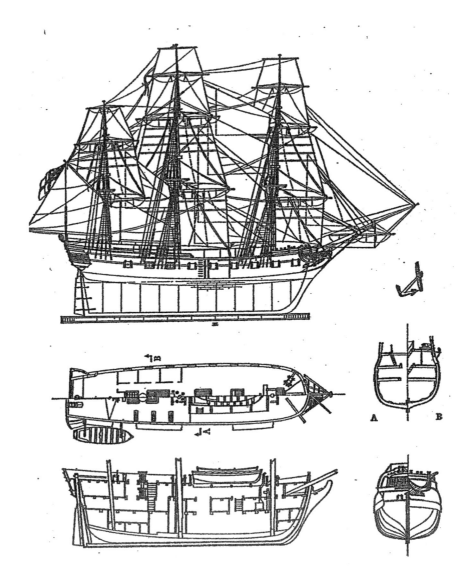

Fig. 2.11
HM Sloop Investigator
(Geeson, N.T., and Sexton, R.T., 'H.M. Sloop Investigator', The Mariners Mirror, vol.56,
no.3, (1970))

31 PRO ADM 95/23-62, Ships' Sailing Qualities
32 PRO ADM 106/3556.127, Sheerness Yard Letters, 1800-1801
33 Ingleton, Geoffrey, C., *Matthew Flinders Navigator and Chartmaker* , p.95
34 PRO ADM 106/3556.66, Sheerness Yard Letters, 1800-1801
35 PRO ADM 106/3556.68, Sheerness Yard Letters, 1800-1801
36 Brown, Anthony, J., *Ill-Starred Captains:Flinders and Baudin*, London, Chatham Publishing, 2001, p.293
37 Ibid, p.53
38 PRO ADM 106/3556.71, Sheerness Yard Letters, 1800-1801
39 Flinders to Ann Chappelle, 18 December 1800: National Maritime Museum, Greenwich (NMM) Manuscript (MS). 60/017. FLI/25.5; Flinders was later promoted to rank of commander with effect from 16 February 1801, Syrett, David and Dinardo R.L., *The Commissioned Sea Officers of the Royal Navy 1660-1815*, p.159.
40 PRO ADM 106/3556.75, Sheerness Yard Letters, 1800-1801
41 PRO ADM 106/3556.82, Sheerness Yard Letters, 1800-1801
42 PRO ADM 106/3556.86, Sheerness Yard Letters, 1800-1801
43 NMM deck plans, Sheerness Yard 1801, Approved 31 January 1801, Reg. no.6224, Box 66I
44 PRO ADM 106/3556.105, Sheerness Yard Letters, 1800-1801
45 Ingleton, Geoffrey, C., *Matthew Flinders Navigator and Chartmaker*, p.96
46 PRO ADM 106/3556.108, Sheerness Yard Letters, 1800-1801
47 PRO ADM 106/3556.116, Sheerness Yard Letters, 1800-1801
48 Ingleton, Geoffrey, C., *Matthew Flinders Navigator and Chartmaker,* p.99
49 PRO ADM 106/3556.117, Sheerness Yard Letters, 1800-1801
50 Austin, K.A., *The Voyage of the Investigator*, p.44
51 Flinders to Ann Chappelle, 6 April 1801: NMM MS. 60/017. FLI/25.7
52 Flinders to Ann Chappelle, 13 April 1801: NMM MS. 60/017. FLI/25.8
53 Tiley, Robert, *Australian Navigators*, p.124
54 May, W. E., *The Man who Named Australia*, The Geographical Magazine (National Geographic), Vol.21(8), pp.306-311, Dec.1948, p.308
55 Ingleton, Geoffrey, C., *Matthew Flinders Navigator and Chartmaker*, p.107
56 Tiley, Robert, *Australian Navigators*, p.124
57 May, W. E., *The Man who Named Australia*, p.308
58 Retter, Catherine & Sinclair, Shirley, *Letters to Ann: the love story of Matthew Flinders and Ann Chappelle*, p.8
59 Ritchie, G.S., *The Admiralty Chart*, p.71
60 Ingleton, Geoffrey, C., *Matthew Flinders Navigator and Chartmaker*, p.110
61 Ibid, p.109
62 Banks' letters to King, Jan 8, Jun 2 1801 and Aug 21 1802: King Papers vol.8
63 Flinders to his wife, 30 June 1801: NMM MS. 60/017. FLI/25.9
64 Flinders to his wife, 7 July 1801: NMM MS. 60/017. FLI/25.11
65 Ingleton, Geoffrey, C., *Matthew Flinders Navigator and Chartmaker*, p.120
66 Ibid, p.121
67 Ibid, p.122
68 Flinders to Banks, 21 October 1801: Br. Library MSS.8100. 32,439, f.45

69   Flinders to Banks, October 1801: Br. Library MSS.8100. 32,439, f.49

70   Monteath, Peter, *The Journal of Seaman Samuel Smith*, p.36

71   Ingleton, Geoffrey, C., *Matthew Flinders Navigator and Chartmaker*, p.133

72   Monteath, Peter, *The Journal of Seaman Samuel Smith*, Adelaide, Corkwood Press, 2002, p.36

73   Ingleton, Geoffrey, C., *Matthew Flinders Navigator and Chartmaker*, p.135

74   Mack, James, D., *Matthew Flinders: 1774 -1814*, Melbourne, Nelson, 1966, p.101

75   Able Seamen J. Little, G. Lewis, J. Hopkins, W. Smith, T. Grindal and R. Williams Ritchie, G.S., *The Admiralty Chart*, p.79

76   Flinders, Matthew, Capt. RN, *A Voyage to Terra Australis*, Vol. 1, p.218

77   Ingleton, Geoffrey, C., *Matthew Flinders Navigator and Chartmaker*, p.157

78   Ritchie, G.S., *The Admiralty Chart*, p.81

79   Flinders to Sir Joseph Banks, 20 May 1802: Br. Library MSS.8100. 32,439, f.54

80   Ritchie, G.S., *The Admiralty Chart*, p.81

81   PRO ADM1/4187, *Lady Nelson* placed under Flinders' command

82   Ingleton, Geoffrey, C., *Matthew Flinders Navigator and Chartmaker*, p.185

83   Ibid, p.188

84   Ibid, p.188

85   Flinders to Sir Joseph Banks, 10 October 1802: Br. Library MSS.8100. 32,439, f.72

86   The *Lady Nelson* had smashed her keel: Mack, James, D., Matthew Flinders: 1774-1814, p.121

87   Mack, James, D., *Matthew Flinders: 1774-1814*, p.126

88   'Wales'-an extra thickness of wood bolted to the sides of a ship where protection is needed. Kemp, Peter, ed., *The Oxford Companion to Ships and the Sea*, p.922

89   'Bends' - a name sometimes applied to the thickest planks on the side of a wooden ship from the waterline or the turn of the bilge upwards; Ibid, p.78

90   Ingleton, Geoffrey, C., *Matthew Flinders Navigator and Chartmaker*, p.210

91   Ritchie, G.S., *The Admiralty Chart*, p.85

92   Flinders, Matthew, Capt. RN, *A Voyage to Terra Australis*, Vol. II, p.142

93   Ingleton, Geoffrey, C., *Matthew Flinders Navigator and Chartmaker*, p.210

94   Flinders to Sir Joseph Banks, 28 March 1803: Br. Library MSS.8100. 32,439, f.82

95   Flinders to his wife, 28 March 1803: NMM MS. 60/017. FLI/25.17

96   Despite Flinders' intention to recover them, the best bower and stream anchors were not retrieved until 1973. The best bower is now in the Maritime Museum at Port Adelaide and the stream anchor in the Western Australia Maritime Museum at Fremantle.

97   Flinders to his wife, 25 June 1803: NMM MS. 60/017. FLI/25.18

98   Colledge J. J., revised by Warlow, Lt-Cdr Ben, *Ships of the Royal Navy*, p.11.

99   Ibid, p.363

100   Geeson, N.T., and Sexton, R.T., *H.M. Sloop Investigator*, The Mariner's Mirror, Vol.56, (1970), p.281; Also as discussed between author and Robert Sexton on 16 December 2003.

Fig. 3.1
*Map of Island of Mauritius
(from a postcard by J. C. Nouralt)*

CHAPTER THREE

Nemesis: Confrontation and Incarceration on the Isle de France (Mauritius)

At dawn on 15 December 1803, those on deck of the schooner *Cumberland* saw the humped outline of the Ile de France emerge from the early gloom of the westerly horizon. The wind was from the southeast and Flinders had given orders for the ship to haul to the north until sighting a distant promontory that could not have been cleared safely in the sea conditions which then prevailed. He then brought the ship about to round the south end of the island instead. Thus began the first day of what was intended to be the briefest of visits, but was to become, for Flinders himself, a detention of nearly seven years during which time his life would change beyond recognition and, sadly, preface his early demise.

The island (Fig. 3.1) had been largely uninhabited, apart from brief visits by Arab seafarers and Portugese navigators in the early sixteenth century, until the Dutch took possession in 1598 and named it Mauritius for Prince Maurice of Orange[1]. During the seventeenth century the Dutch East India Company had established a settlement, but in 1710 they departed and it became a haven for pirates until annexed by Dufresne d'Arsel for France in 1715 who took occupation and renamed it Ile de France[2]. During the eighteenth century the population grew, business and plantations flourished (aided by some 63,000 African slaves)[3], and a fortified naval base was established at Port Louis. The island played a key role in the colonial wars fought by the major European powers, despite its remote location. It was a principal base for the support of campaigns against the British in India, for the harassment of British maritime trade, for French exploration in the Far East and a haven for privateers. Even the impact of the French Revolution had only a slight effect on the economy and way of life of the mainly royalist islanders, as Flinders was to discover.

On 17 August 1803 General Decaen, with a small force, sailed into Port Louis from Pondicherry in India[4], with the firm intention of submitting 'les iles rebelles'[5] to the rule of Napoleon's consular government as the new Governor General[6]. A successful military man, a strategist with legal training who saw himself as the Napoleon of the Indian Ocean and possibly of the Pacific, the potential 'Emperor' of the antipodean world, he had no hesitation in displaying his 'imperial despotic' style of rule. Like Flinders he dreamed of

Fig. 3.2

*Baie du Cap
(photograph by
author, October
2003)*

immortality, not as a scientist or explorer, but as a conquering soldier of his most hated enemies, the English[7]. Away from the European battlefields it was at Ile de France that Decaen meant to prepare, for himself, a place among the 'immortals' by destroying British source wealth in the Indian Ocean. It would be his contribution to France's war efforts on the sub-continent. His plan was well constructed; the Ile de France would be the centre of action, and he would be the mastermind directing the operations. As representative of the First Consul in the Indian Ocean, and the bearer of his instructions, he would be equal to Napoleon in his determination to combine the forces of the Asian world against the common enemy, England[8]. He may even have seen himself as seceding Napoleon in Asia.

All this, including the resumption of hostilities between the two powers, was unknown to Flinders as he closed the island some four months later. He initially hoisted the French flag at the masthead, believing this to be the signal for a pilot, as well as British colours. He then followed a small schooner along the coast and into a little cove, Baie du Cap[9], in the belief that it had offered piloting services[10]. (Figs. 3.2 and 3.3) It was only when he was anchored he discovered that Britain and France were again at war. His worries were exacerbated by his passport, which he could not read as it was in French; its wording had been briefly explained to him before he'd sailed from England in 1801, but critically, it only applied to the *Investigator*, not the *Cumberland*. On discovering that *le Géographe* and *le Naturaliste* from Baudin's French expedition were still in Port Louis, although Baudin himself had died that September[11], he felt confident that others from those ships would vouch for him following their kind treatment from Governor King when they had put into Port Jackson. At that time Baudin had written a letter of introduction, which he had personally given to King, for use by Flinders should he ever need assistance at the Ile de France. The letter, forgotten or probably mislaid, was never used but discovered many years later among Governor King's papers[12]. With this in mind he sailed up the western coast to Port Louis with a French pilot onboard expecting the kindest reception from the Governor of Mauritius[13].

Up to this point in his life Flinders had, despite some errors of judgement, met the right people and been in the right places at the right time. Fate had now shifted his destiny so that he found himself in the wrong place with the wrong people - although arguably still at the right time. The events that had allowed him to seek his fame through science were linked to trade, power and wealth. It was his direct but unwitting involvement in the political machinations of that time that would now throw him at the feet and mercy of

Fig. 3.3
Memorial at Baie du Cap
(photograph by Sheryl Chandler, Flinder University, November 2003)

his nemesis, the competing fierce and hungry French hegemony. Furthermore, unbeknown to Flinders, François Péron the naturalist from *le Géographe*[15], had filed a report with Decaen on Port Jackson's defences but, more specifically, on the expedition of discovery by Flinders towards the expansionist policies of the British in the Indian and Pacific Oceans[16]. Flinders would have had little concept of how fragile his position was. He had sailed into an enemy port, in a vessel entirely inconsistent with, and unfit for, the nature of his expedition, without a single scientist or evidence of their work, without a valid passport, carrying classified dispatches, in breach of the terms of the passport, which he had not thought to dispose of over the ship's side[17]. He was about to commit another horrendous blunder. He was going to need every ounce of tact and diplomacy to extricate himself and his ship from the situation. Regrettably, he would prove demonstrably to have had very little of either.

Upon his arrival in Port Louis on 17 December Flinders wrote in his diary:

> …we got to anchor at the entrance of Port Louis, near the ship which, I had hoped, might be le Géographe; but Captain Melius had sailed for France on the preceding day[18].

He was taken immediately to see Decaen, who kept him waiting for some time. While being detained he chatted amicably, but in broken English with some French officers who enquired if he knew of a 'Monsieur Flinedare', not recognising his own name he was to write in his journal later:

> …of which , to their surprise I knew nothing, but afterwards found it to be my own name they so pronounced[19].

This information would have been passed onto Decaen before he saw Flinders.

After a lengthy delay Flinders was admitted to Decaen's presence, whereupon he began to immerse himself into probably the most intractable position of his life because of his arrogant and bellicose attitude. A feeling of intense hostility immediately flared up between the two men when Flinders refused to remove his hat, a disrespectful stance of the time, particularly from a man in such a tenuous position. Due to their being at crossed purposes politically, because the General was almost certainly still smarting from the treatment he had received at the hands of the British at Pondicherry, and not least because of the report he had recently read from Péron, Flinders was suspected of being an imposter and his passport was demanded without ceremony. In all probability the General would also have been acquainted with the intrusion carried out by Mr Robbins, the previous captain of the *Cumberland*, into the hydrographic work of Baudin off King Island on the south coast of Australia[20]. He therefore demanded to see the order permitting Flinders to put in at Ile de France in addition to the passport. On being told that there was none Decaen lost what little patience he possessed and began shouting and gesticulating, in typical Gallic fashion, finally using the words, '…you are imposing on me, Sir.'[21]

Thus the stage was set for the unfolding of a tragedy in which the two protagonists, equally animated by the passionate desire to make for themselves a great name in history, equally devoted to the cause of their countries, gradually lost control of events until Nemesis dispensed her final fatal blow. Both characters in presence possessed outstanding qualities, but so complex was the combination of events in which they became intertwined that the perception of their personalities became distorted. The world at large is at a loss until the end of the drama, to discover who of the two men plays the part of the hero or that of the villain.

After a brief period, during which Flinders' passport[22] was re-examined and his explanations grudgingly accepted, he was directed to collect his charts and journals from the ship for examination in order to confirm that the neutrality under which he sailed had not been violated. In the case of the passport it was established that it was issued both in the name of the ship, *Investigator*, and in the name of its commander, Flinders, and protection was extended to the ship, her officers, crew and cargo for the duration of the voyage[23].

The following day, Sunday 18 December, was that which Flinders would live to rue for the remainder of his short life. No doubt he was still seething and fairly tired following further questioning by Decaen's staff officers when he was invited to dine with the Captain-General and his wife. Inexplicably and, as it would turn out, disastrously, he refused on the grounds that he had already dined. It was only 5 pm, and he had spent the afternoon being quizzed. Colonel Monistrol, Decaen's aide-de-camp, who had brought the invitation tried to persuade him to at least appear at the table out of courtesy to Madame Decaen to no avail. Flinders replied that:

> …under my present situation and treatment, it was impossible; when they should be changed, - when I should be at liberty, if his excellency thought it proper to invite me, I should be flattered by it, and accept his invitation with pleasure…[24]

Thus by standing on his dignity as an English naval officer who considered that he had been grossly insulted in both his public and private character, he missed the opportunity to ameliorate what was becoming a tense international incident with quiet, even genial conversation, over a glass of good wine with Decaen and his lady. He would have found himself in the presence of a man who could be kind-hearted and entertaining when not provoked, and of a charming French lady. He would have been able to hold them spellbound with the stories of his adventures in the *Providence* and the *Investigator* thus demonstrating his *bona fides* completely. It would have been surprising if Decaen, with his background, would not have been impressed. But Flinders was angry; perhaps justifiably, but unfortunately angry nevertheless and he lost his chance[25]. He wrote in his narrative that he believed the invitation to be a trick:

> ...the air of an experiment, to ascertain whether I really was a commander in the British Navy; and had the invitation been accepted without explanation or a change of treatment, an inference might have been drawn that the change of imposture was well founded; but in any case, having been grossly insulted ..., I could not debase the situation I had the honour to hold by a tacit submission[26].

In short, he believed that, under the circumstances, to accept the invitation to dinner would have been so out of character for an English naval officer it would have confirmed him to be a spy. It apparently never occurred to Flinders that the invitation may well have been intended as an honour extended to an enemy and an officer, albeit of inferior rank, and possibly an attempt to recompense him for the poor treatment he had received thus far. It was unlikely that Decaen's gesture concealed any deep ulterior motive; after all, he would have had other means of extracting information. This was a dangerous snub. Winston Churchill wrote, nearly a century later:

> ...the position of a prisoner of war is painful and humiliating... all military pride, all independence of spirit must be put aside. These may carried to the grave, but not into captivity[27].

However, Flinders effectively slammed the door on the priceless opportunity to meet Decaen on a social level, which might have changed the course of events which was to thwart both men's ambitions[28]. Had he acknowledged that some deference was due to the official head of the colony of a foreign power with whom his own country was at war, and accepted the invitation with grace, his ensuing troubles would almost certainly have been avoided. As it was, the opportunity to ease the misunderstanding never occurred again, each man obstinately stood his own ground and even hardened his attitude towards the other.

The following day, by which time Decaen had had time to study Flinders' papers and despatches, the situation was exacerbated by the discovery of the passage near the end of volume III of the journal, setting out amongst other reasons for calling at the Ile de France:

> ...acquiring a knowledge of the periodical winds and weather there;-of the port and the present state of the French colony; and how far it or its dependencies in Madagasgar may be useful to Port Jackson[29].

More than any other single factor, and there were others of significance in the despatches, that one sentence destroyed Flinders' case. It was the evidence upon which Decaen built his case for detaining him. Despite all pleas of innocence, all reference to the support given to Baudin at Port Jackson, all records of exploration, Decaen then saw nothing but espionage. Everything else was mere façade[30]. He then charged Flinders explicitly with violating his neutrality and invalidating his passport and referred the matter to Denis Descrès, the Minister of Marine and Colonies, in Paris[31].

Once again Flinders' stubborn pig-headiness and belief in his own self-righteousness worked against him. On 25 December he wrote to Decaen in which he attempted to demonstrate the futility of the General's accusation but unfortunately lacked the civility and diplomacy necessary in such a delicate situation:

> ...I cannot think that an officer of your rank and judgement can act so ungentlemanlike or so unguardedly, as to make such a declaration without proof, unless his reason has been blinded by a passion, or a previous determination that it should be so[32].

Flinders was to explain his lack of civility when writing up his journal some ten years later:

> ...as my demand was to obtain common justice, an adulatory style did not seem proper, more especially when addressed to a Republican who must despise it. My rights had been invaded, and I used the language natural to a man so circumstanced[33].

The answer from the General was immediate and without room for appeal:

> ...extraordinary as it was inconsiderate, to depart from Port Jackson in the *Cumberland* more to give proof of officious zeal, more for the private interests of Great Britain than for what had induced the French Government to give you a passport, which I shall unfold at a proper opportunity, had already given me an idea of your character, but this letter overstepping all the bounds of civility, obliges me to tell you until the general opinion judges of your faults or mine, to cease all correspondence tending to demonstrate the justice of your cause, since you know so little how to preserve the rules of civility[34].

Decaen was never to depart from this stand and ingeniously continued inventing pretexts to detain him as a prisoner, even after Napoleon authorised his release[35], while Flinders kept up a barrage of appeals to Decaen, which were ignored, and to the British and French governments for his liberation[36].

Decaen commented that Flinders was a 'trop vif' -'a smart alec' while Flinders himself accused the governor of being an egotist and a tyrant. In his journal he later wrote describing Decaen's attitude with the pertinent remark, '...embarrassment sheltering itself under despotic power'[37].

That Flinders still believed this when he wrote his narrative some ten years later, gives not only an indication of the extent of his arrogance[38], but also that he felt so strongly the injustice dealt him, the scar remained. His frustration, disappointment and exhaustion at the time were not in doubt, but his explanation a decade later revealed, even with the benefit of hindsight, little recognition of the tenuous position he had been in. Regrettably it did suggest that, despite his brilliance as a navigator and cartographer, he was arrogant and excessively proud, with a view of his own importance beyond that of anyone else's, and a failing to appreciate the views of others which did not align with his own. It was quite possibly this unfortunate quality which had failed to impress Earl St. Vincent some three years earlier as the *Investigator* was about to set sail on the voyage of discovery. It had also caused some disquiet in Admiralty circles in regard to the youth and inexperience of the sloop's commander[39].

It is important to remember that he was relatively young, being not yet thirty, and inexperienced in the ways of world politics when all this happened. Once the dreadful machinations of the situation had been set in motion they would grind this sanguine young man into a white-haired melancholic who would on more than one occasion come very close to the point of breakdown before he was eventually released[40].

While it was alleged that Flinders disregarded all the rules of politeness, it must be said that only an intense feeling of resentment against his initial reception on arrival at the Ile de France might have caused his habitually courteous disposition to become unhinged. Despite his impetuous nature, he was noted for his gentle manner in his relations with all he came into contact with, showing respect for authority and consideration for his subordinates. He appeared to be a popular and able commander of the *Investigator*. A study of his letters, journals and other papers from throughout his career fail to reveal any other instance of even a temporary deviation from perfect courtesy. Even in this case the fault was perhaps not entirely his, there was sufficient aggravation to incite anger in an honest man. Nevertheless, the solitary instance of a natural flame of anger cannot be ignored or minimised in view of the long train of miserable consequences to which it led[41].

However, Flinders had never really had to interact with others on equal terms since his appointment to the *Investigator*. With the powerful Banks as his patron he had not needed to concern himself with the thoughts, and in particular any objections of others, including Admiralty, before he embarked

Fig. 3.4
Portrait of Charles Isodore Mathieu Decaen, c. 1804-1810
(courtesy of Mauritius Museums Council, Mauritius)

on the voyage. In the ship, as its commander, he wielded, and had the full authority and discipline of the Royal Navy to reinforce, his orders. At Port Jackson, Governor King - also dependent on Banks' support - was sympathetic to all his requirements, although King was to unwittingly exacerbate his problems at the Ile de France. It was only at Mauritius that Flinders for the first time had to deal with people for whom his connections meant nothing. It was also most likely that Flinders did not understand just who and how powerful Decaen was. Despite his apparent lack of years, he was actually five years older than Flinders, the same age as Napoleon, his mentor[42]. Decaen was no petty provincial governor (Fig. 3.4), but a man personally selected by Napoleon to wrest India from the British and then rule the sub-continent. In common with Flinders, it was bad timing and world politics which had placed him on the island, and it would be world politics which would bring about the demise of both men[43].

That Flinders was on the Ile de France at all was the culmination of a series of disasters, exacerbated by his determination to return to England with his charts and his indomitable spirit in the face of adversity. Governor Philip Gidley King of New South Wales, while a strong supporter of Flinders, had expressed caution over the course of the passage back to England, and yet was to prove the unwitting agent of disaster.

Following the fateful condemnation of the *Investigator* at Port Jackson, King persuaded Flinders to return to England as a passenger in the supply ship *Porpoise*[44]. It was at this time that Flinders had the premonition of impending disaster. In fact, ill luck was to dog him for the remainder of his life, when he noted for his report to the Admiralty:

> …since the accomplishment of the survey was an object so near to my heart that could I have foreseen the train of ills that were to follow the decay of the Investigator and prevent the survey being resumed, and had my existence depended upon the expression of a wish, I do not know that it would have received utterance; but Infinite Wisdom has, in infinite mercy, reserved the knowledge of futurity to itself[45].

A week after sailing the *Porpoise* was wrecked, but again Flinders' bravery and indomitable spirit saw him organise the rescue of his crew to a dry sandbank with provisions before, with six men, he set off in a cutter to return to Port Jackson, arriving fourteen days later. Astounded, Governor King wrote in an official letter,

> …I could not sufficiently commend your voluntary services, and those who came with you, in undertaking a voyage of 700 miles in an open boat to procure relief for our friends now on the reef[46].

Flinders and King quickly agreed upon a plan for the relief of the wrecked crew, a mission which was led and accomplished by Flinders before he set sail a second time for England in the 29-ton schooner *Cumberland*. Built in Port Jackson for local work the vessel was hardly stronger than a canal barge and unsuitable for ocean navigation, which made it necessary to stop at every convenient port on the voyage for running repairs, water and other refreshment. The orders given to Flinders were set out in a letter from Governor King dated 17 September 1803:

> ... you will proceed to England by the route you judge most advisable and beneficial for His Majesty's service. On your arrival in London you will deliver my letters to the Admiralty and the Principal Secretary of State for Colonies[47].

King left the detail of the choice of route to Flinders but, while objecting to Mauritius, although at the time he was unaware of the breakdown of the Treaty of Amiens and the resumption of hostilities, he did not wish to encourage communications between the French colony and Port Jackson. It was therefore somewhat surprising that while he left the final decision to Flinders' judgement, he entrusted him with two letters for the Governor of Mauritius. He was also unaware that General Decaen had replaced the more moderate Governor Magallon that August[48]. Flinders, having been cautioned against laying anchor at Mauritius and being conscious that he might have to answer before a court martial for going against a superior officer's instructions, thought it a wise precaution to record his reasons for calling there in his journal. In addition to that of noting information appertaining to the wind, weather and the port and its disposition, these were three-fold:

1. The necessity of caulking the schooner and of refitting the pumps before attempting to round the Cape of Good Hope;
2. The hope of obtaining passage in a ship bound for Europe that he might have returned to present his charts and journals to the Admiralty with the minimum of delay;
3. In the event that England was again at war with France, ...a French passport would not be considered by the Dutch government at the Cape[49].

While King was unaware of the resumption of hostilities between the two nations, it was at best naive of him to entrust despatches of a military nature to the commander of a scientific expedition, which was protected by a passport of neutrality from the potential enemy. He later conceded his indiscretion in a letter to Decaen written on 5 June 1805 pleading for the release of Flinders:

> ...en se présentant à vous comme gouverneur de l'Ile de France, lorsqu'il s'attendait du moins à etre traité comme gallant homme, dans la situation où il a paru il fut traité à tout égard comme espion excepté qu'il n'as pas été exécuté comme tel[50].

Conversely Flinders revealed his naivety or carelessness when he infringed the specific rules prescribed for those appointed in command of protected expeditions. The orders, which he had been given by the Admiralty before leaving England in 1801, had contained specific instructions:

> ...not to take letters or packets other than as you may receive from this office or the office of his Majesty's Secretary of State[51].

There are two possible explanations for this transgression. Either Flinders was totally ignorant of the contents of King's despatches which, if true, was again a weakness on his part or, the view taken by Decaen, that he had received secret instructions, although there was no evidence of such in the despatches, which corresponded with the aims and views expressed in the documents. But there was no evidence of secret instructions amongst the documents confiscated by Decaen. After having scrutinised the papers Decaen was convinced that he had the proof of King's aggressive intentions against the Ile de France[52] and held the evidence which proved that Flinders, while risking his life in a small boat to deliver them, had infringed the terms of his passport.

Flinders, the impetuous young commander anxious to achieve fame and world-wide recognition was, at that time, scarcely aware that he was about to be detained for an indeterminate length of time, '...pour la défense des intérêts de l'Etat'[53] The long frustrating years were to quench his aspirations, cool his ambition and weaken his already ailing physical well-being. Fortunately he was not worn down in his determination to free himself at all costs in order that he could return to record the account of his voyage to Terra Australis, which he eventually did:

> ...some proof that while Decaen and Mauritius held the man, the mind and the spirit were unconfined[54].

The case of Flinders constituted one of the first great international incidents in the world at the beginning of the nineteenth century. Protests against his detention were made from Sydney to Paris and from India to London. One reason at least for his prolonged incarceration at 'Le Refuge', Wilhelms Plaines, (Fig. 3.5) was precisely because he had become a diplomatic pawn in world politics. This in part, at least, explains why little was done to extricate him from Decaen's clutches until the British forces had been assembled and were ready to take the island some six and a half years later in 1810. Flinders was a highly skilled and trained cartographer and, as such, a threat to the security of the French colony of the Ile de France. With the aid of a few elementary tools he was more than capable of making a representation of the whole island, its roads, mountain topography and, most crucially, its coastline with its bays and coves suitable for an invasion force. Since this was what the French themselves had been doing while the ships of Nicolas Baudin's expedition had been in Port Jackson, Decaen, the rationalist, had Flinders politically marked down[55]. That Flinders failed to adjust to the situation at the time, and even ten years later by which time peace had been restored, albeit briefly, following Napoleon's exile to Elba, suggests character traits such as immaturity, stubbornness and insensitivity with perhaps a generous dose of ambition as the catalyst for disaster.

Fig. 3.5
Memorial at La Marie, Vacoas, Plaines Wilhelms (site of 'Le Refuge')
(photography by author, October 2003)

1   Estensen, Miriam, The Life of Matthew Flinders, Crows Nest NSW, Allen & Unwin, 2003, p.312

2   Pineo, Huguette, Ly-Tio-Fane, In the Grips of the Eagle: Matthew Flinders at Ile de France, 1803- 1810, Mauritius, Mahatma Gandhi Institute, 1988, p.5

3   Estensen, Miriam, The Life of Matthew Flinders, p.313

4   Decaen had failed to secure the surrender of Pondicherry from the British as the Treaty of Amiens was about to be repudiated; Pineo, Huguette, Ly-Tio-Fane, In the Grips of the Eagle: Matthew Flinders at Ile de France, 1803- 1810, p.50.

5   'the rebel islanders'

6   Pineo, Huguette, Ly-Tio-Fane, In the Grips of the Eagle: Matthew Flinders at Ile de France, 1803- 1810, p.35

7   Gertsakis, Elizabeth, The Lost Letters of Ann Chappelle Flinders, Adelaide, Flinders University, 2002, p.6

8   Pineo, Huguette, Ly-Tio-Fane, In the Grips of the Eagle: Matthew Flinders at Ile de France, 1803- 1810, p.56

9   Ibid, p.68

10   McCrae, G.G., Geographical discoveries and explorers of the 18th century and earlier part of the 19th century - La Perouse and Baudin in New South Wales, and Flinders in Mauritius: their experience at the hands of colonial officials, Royal Geographic Society, Victoria, Vol.29, pp.1-19, 1912, p.9. Flinders University Library Special Collection EPH 7051

11   Tiley, Robert, Australian Navigators, Sydney, Kangaroo Press, 2002, p.180

12   McCrae, Geographical discoveries and explorers of the eighteenth century ..., p.6.

13   Pineo, Huguette, Ly-Tio-Fane, In the Grips of the Eagle: Matthew Flinders at Ile de France, 1803- 1810, p.69

14   Gertsakis, Elizabeth, The Lost Letters of Ann Chappelle Flinders, p.7

15   Pineo, Huguette, Ly-Tio-Fane, In the Grips of the Eagle: Matthew Flinders at Ile de France, 1803- 1810, p.33

16   Scott, Ernest, The Life of Matthew Flinders, Sydney, Harper Collins, 2001 (1914) p.459

17   Tiley, Robert, Australian Navigators, p.184

18   Flinders, Matthew, A Voyage to Terra Australis, 2 Vols, atlas, London, G & W Nicol, 1814, Vol.2 p.359

19   Ibid, p.360

20   Pineo, Huguette, Ly-Tio-Fane, In the Grips of the Eagle: Matthew Flinders at Ile de France, 1803- 1810, p.72

21   Flinders, Matthew, A Voyage to Terra Australis, Vol.2, p.360

22   Flinders' passport issued on orders of the First Consul, dated 23rd May 1801, signed by Forfait, Minister of Marine and Colonies; NMM Greenwich MS. 60/017, FLI/3.1.

23   Mault, A, Detention of Flinders at Mauritius, Royal Society of Tasmania, Paper 18, pp.121-124. 1889, p.121; Flinders University Library Special Collection, EPH 7021

24   Flinders, Matthew, A Voyage to Terra Australis, p.363

25   Scott, Ernest, The Life of Matthew Flinders, p.237

26   Flinders, Matthew, A Voyage to Terra Australis, p.364

27   Churchill, Winston, S., London to Ladysmith, (New York, 1900), p.96

28   Pineo, Huguette, Ly-Tio-Fane, In the Grips of the Eagle: Matthew Flinders at Ile de

France, 1803- 1810, p.74

29 Flinders, Matthew, Private Diary (Journal), Dec.17th 1803-July 4th 1814, the Mitchell Library-State Library of New South Wales, Sydney, Vol.III, p.95

30 Mack, James D., Matthew Flinders: 1774-1814, Melbourne, Nelson, 1966, p.181

31 Decaen, General C, Report on the Detention of Flinders, Proceedings of the Royal Geographic Society of Australasia, Vol.12, 1910-1911, pp.36-41; Flinders University Library Special Collection, EPH 7023.

32 Flinders, Matthew, Private Diary (Journal), 17 December 1803-4 July 1814, Vol.II, p.373.

33 Ibid, p.377

34 Ibid, p.374

35 Order for the liberation of Flinders received by Banks 20 September 1806, sent from France two months earlier; Banks' Papers, Vol.16, Misc. Correspondence, p.167; Order for liberation of Flinders, signed by Napoleon, 5 May 1809, forwarded by Banks and delivered under flag of truce to Decaen, who ignored, probably due to instructions from another department of French Government, Banks' Papers.

36 PRO. ADM1/4197 4 September 1804; Flinders' account of his detention at the Ile de France.

37 Flinders, Matthew, Private Diary (Journal), Dec.17th 1803-July 4th 1814, p.375

38 Tiley, Robert, Australian Navigators, p.187

39 Ibid.

40 Purdon, N., Matthew Flinders: the investigator of himself, The Adelaide Review, pp.10-11, January 1987; Flinders University Library Special Collection, EPH 9502

41 Scott, Ernest, The Life of Matthew Flinders, p.239

42 Tiley, Robert, Australian Navigators, p.187

43 Ibid.

44 Pineo, Huguette, Ly-Tio-Fane, In the Grips of the Eagle: Matthew Flinders at Ile de France, 1803- 1810, p.64

45 PRO. ADM. 7/707, Flinders' Narrative of Imprisonment by French, July 1806; Pineo, Huguette, Ly-Tio-Fane, In the Grips of the Eagle: Matthew Flinders at Ile de France, 1803- 1810, p.64.

46 Flinders, Matthew, A Voyage to Terra Australis, p.324

47 Pineo, Huguette, Ly-Tio-Fane, In the Grips of the Eagle: Matthew Flinders at Ile de France, 1803- 1810, p.65

48 Ibid, p.53

49 Flinders, Matthew, Private Diary (Journal), Dec.17th 1803-July 4th 1814, p.351

50 Pineo, Huguette, Ly-Tio-Fane, In the Grips of the Eagle: Matthew Flinders at Ile de France, 1803- 1810, p.75; Translation: ...'by introducing himself [Flinders] to you [Decaen] as governor of the region of the Ile de France, when he was expecting to be treated like a gentleman, in the situation he appeared in he has been treated under any aspect as a spy except he hasn't been executed as such'.

51 Ibid.

52 Ibid, p.77

53 Ibid, p.84, 'In the interests of the State'

54 Flinders, Matthew, A Biographical Tribute to Trim, Sydney, Harper & Collins, 1997.

55 Purdon, N., Matthew Flinders: the investigator of himself, The Adelaide Review, pp.10-11, January 1987; Flinders University Library Special Collection, EPH 9502.

Statue of Matthew Flinders on North Terrace, Adelaide
(photograph by author, November 2003)

Conclusion

Flinders was finally released, having given his parole not to engage in warlike activities against the French, and sailed from Mauritius in the cartel *Harriet*, later transferring to the sloop *Otter*, on 13 June 1810. However, he did not arrive back in England until 24 October following a seven-week delay at Cape Town where he transferred to the schooner *Olympia* following being de-briefed by Vice-Admiral Bertie who was planning the invasion of the Ile de France. Before giving any information, Flinders, despite his treatment by Decaen, demonstrated his integrity when he protested that his parole included the promise:

> ...not to act in any service which might be considered directly or indirectly hostile to France or its allies, during the course of the present war[1].

Back in London he reported immediately to the Admiralty, wrote to Banks[2] and was reunited with Ann after a separation of nine years and three months[3], a totally different man physically, if not mentally. Bouts of scurvy and the increasing incidents of his 'gravelly' complaint, the legacy of his youth in Tahiti which would now return with fatal consequences, had severely compromised his well-being. Although only thirty-six, his once dark hair had turned white and he looked fifty.

So many of Flinders' career aspirations were not so much dashed as only half-fulfilled; not least his circumnavigation of Terra Australis in the *Investigator*. Whatever the reasons for his mission being aborted, none was as significant and debilitating as the poor state of repair and un-seaworthiness of his ship. He either failed to see, or chose to turn a 'blind-eye', to the shortcomings of the ship which he held together more by willpower and sheer determination than pumping and caulking for over two years, while the Admiralty Lords may have been less than sincere in their support for the expedition. Now he found that the long overdue promotion to post-captain promised by Lord Spencer back in 1801[4], while approved[5], could not be back-dated earlier than 7 May 1810 due to his incarceration on Mauritius and the change of First Lord, now Sir Joseph Yorke, without setting a precedent[6]. Decaen had unwittingly struck another blow which was to remain a cause of bitterness for the rest of his life. Furthermore, being unfit for sea service due to ill-health, he was placed on half-pay of four shillings per day, albeit back-dated to 18 December 1803, until his death[7]. The East India Company behaved rather more agreeably when in November 1810 their Court of Directors ordered a warrant to be made out to Flinders for the £600 promised in March 1801[8].

Undeterred, Flinders now set about the work of preparing his journal and charts for publication, which would take three years to complete. During this time he was also to carry out important work on magnetic compass deviation and corrections to the lunar tables in the Nautical Almanac[9]. He devoted all his time and remaining energy to the completion of his account of the first circumnavigation of Terra Australis but, by the end of 1813, his 'gravelly' complaint - the still totally undiagnosed kidney infection - returned with a vengeance[10]. By March 1814 he was finding it almost impossible to work, the surgeon was visiting every day, but he never lost the will to squeeze every drop from every day. He breathed his last on 19 July 1814 aged forty years and four months, the same day that his journal came off the press. Tragedy even followed him to the grave, for St. James' churchyard, where he was buried, was redeveloped later in the nineteenth century, and his tomb, with his bones, were displaced[11]. Flinders died in agony. His stoicism and indomitable spirit were to be admired - a quality in him which had been present through most of his life, but was most evident in the latter years during his illness. He was a man with an extraordinary mind and surveying skill. However, he was a slave to his own stubbornness, pride and obstinacy, and suffered for it. He was, nevertheless, a zealous and tenacious officer who did the utmost for his country[12].

Sidney Baker, in his book[13], sets out to reveal the inevitability of Flinders' tragic end through a framework of psychoanalysis[14], and that his personality defects were the cause of all his problems. Even his title, 'My Own Destroyer', has been taken from Defoe's *Robinson Crusoe*, which he considers to be Flinders' theme text. 'I was born to be my own destroyer' are the words of the desert island castaway, Robinson Crusoe, and incidentally the book which Flinders read as a boy which set him on his career in the Navy, much against his father's wishes[15]. Baker believed that Flinders' early disagreement with his father, and other clashes with authority, notably Bligh, induced a resentment against autocratic direction which surfaced in his confrontation with Decaen. While this cannot easily be disputed, in view of what occurred, it cannot be overlooked that history is full of 'ifs', instances when alternatives might have altered the course of history. Many significant 'ifs' arise in examining the misfortunes of Matthew Flinders, the three most significant are:

IF he had not indulged in the pleasures offered by the ladies of Tahiti he would almost certainly have not contracted the kidney disease, which finally killed him. By the same token, IF the Investigator had not leaked like a 'sieve' he would almost certainly have completed his mission to chart the entire coast of Terra Australis and not had to attempt to return to England in the Cumberland, via Mauritius; Additionally, IF he had accepted Madame Decaen's invitation to dine he would almost certainly not have been detained at the Ile de France for as long as six and a half years[17].

But all this is hypothetical and contrary to the facts.

Whatever his shortcomings, and Flinders was a flawed human being, he remained an indomitable man of action and an outstanding scientist, navigator and surveyor. Furthermore, he possessed the two key attributes required of a seaman - courage and professional ability. Courage defined as to have the nerve to do what must be done, he once wrote:

...the commander who proposes to make the experiment, must not, however, be one who throws his ship's head round in a hurry, so soon as breakers are announced from aloft; if he do not feel his nerves are strong enough to thread the needle, as it is called, amongst the reefs, whilst he directs the steerage from the mast head, I would strongly recommend him not to approach this part of New South Wales[18].

His professional ability, or expertise, was born of experience, but some have it, some do not; and some are better than others. Flinders was superb, and he should now be allowed to take his place alongside Bligh, Cook and Nelson in the maritime Pantheon.

Endnotes

1   Flinders, Matthew, *A Voyage to Terra Australis*, Vol.II, 2 Vols. atlas, London, G & W Nicol, 1814, p.482

2   'I have the happiness to inform you of my arrival...': Flinders to Banks, 25 October 1810: B.L. MSS. 32439.332

3   Flinders, Matthew, *A Voyage to Terra Australis*, Vol.II, p.494

4   Tiley, Robert, *Australian Navigators*, Sydney, Kangaroo Press, 2002, p.204

5   National Maritime Museum, Greenwich, Manuscript 60/017, FLI/3 and FLI/5

6   Mack, James D., *Matthew Flinders: 1774-1814*, Melbourne, Nelson, 1966, p.217

7   Ibid, p.218

8   Ibid, note 17

9   May, Cdr. W.E., RN. *The History of the Magnetic Compass*, M.M. vol.38, no.3, (1952), pp. 210-222

10 Tiley, Robert, A*ustralian Navigators*, p.210

11 Buried St. James', Hampstead Road but no record has been found of where his bones may have been moved to following re-development of graveyard; Pineo, Huguette, Ly-Tio-Fane, *In the Grips of the Eagle: Matthew Flinders at Ile de France, 1803-1810*, Mauritius, Mahatma Gandhi Institute, 1988, p.178; Scott, Ernest, *The Life of Matthew Flinders*, Sydney, Harper Collins, 2001 (1914), p.286

12 Tiley, Robert, *Australian Navigators*, p.217

13 Baker, Sidney J., *My Own Destroyer*: A Biography of Matthew Flinders, Explorer and Navigator, Sydney, Currawong, 1962

14 Ellis, M.H., *Psycho-analysing Matthew Flinders*, (review of Baker, S.J., *My Own Destroyer*), The Bulletin, 13 October 1962, pp.38-39; Flinders University Library Special Collec

15 Mack, James D., *Matthew Flinders*: 1774-1814, p.5; From his deathbed Flinders asked for his name to be added to the list of subscribers to the new edition of Robinson Crusoe: 'Biographical Memoir of Matthew Flinders, R.N.', Naval Chronicle, Vol. XXXII, (July-August 1814), p.190; Flinders University Library Special Collection, EPH 7002

16 Russell, R. W., *Matthew Flinders-The Ifs of History*, Adelaide, Flinders University, 1979, p.94

17 Ibid, p.97

18 Flinders, Matthew, *A Voyage to Terra Australis*, Vol. II, p.104

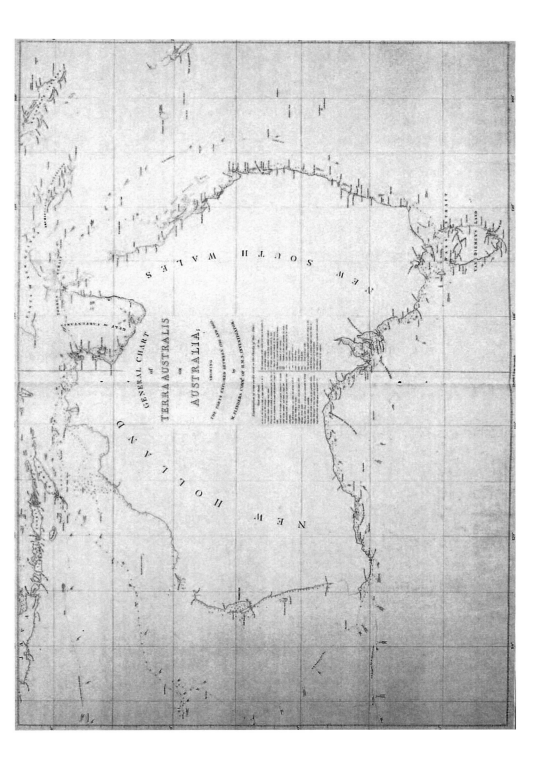

Appendix A - Chronology:
Life of Matthew Flinders
World Events have been italicised

1774   16 March - Born, Donington, Lincolnshire

1775-83   *War of American Independence; France supports rebels; Britain loses sovereignty over American colonies*

1778   *American alliance with France*

1779   22 May - sister Susanna, born
Spain declares War on England

1780   26 January - entered at Mr. Whitehead's School for reading only.

1781   4 March - begins writing at Mr.Whitehead's.
British surrender to America at Yorktown

1783   23 March - mother dies
American War of Independence ends - Peace of Versailles
William Pitt the Younger becomes PM

1785   December - Matthew is reported to be learning well, particularly Latin.

1786   24 July - starts at the Reverend Shingler's Boarding School.

1787   December - returns from School to assist his father in the family business.

1788   *First Fleet of British colonists arrives in Botany Bay; settlement established at Sydney Cove, Port Jackson, on 26 January*

1789   23 October - joins Royal Navy, entered on books of HMS *Alert* as a lieutenant's servant (does not join)
April - Mutiny on the Bounty
Storming of Bastille

1790   17 May - joins HMS *Scipio* as able-seaman rate for cruise with Captain Pasley
20 July - joins HMS *Bellerophon* as Able-seaman rate
31 July - junior midshipman under Pasley

1791	14 April - joins HMS *Dictator* as junior midshipman 8 May - joins HMS *Providence* as midshipman under Captain William Bligh for second 'breadfruit' voyage
1793	August returns to England 7 September - re-joins the *Bellerophon* as able-seaman rate 1 October - senior midshipman *Execution of Louis XVI: French Revolutionary War starts* *France declares War on England*
1794	June - serving in HMS *Bellerophon* at 'Battle of the Glorious First of June' against French 11 August - joins HMS *Reliance* as Masters mate
1795	First expedition in the *Tom Thumb* with George Bass - to Botany Bay and the George's River 25 November - promoted acting-lieutenant in the *Reliance*
1796	March - second expedition with George Bass in the *Tom Thumb II* - to south coast of New South Wales *Spain declares War on England*
1797	December - Bass's whaleboat journey establishes strong likelihood of the existence of a strait between Van Diemen's Land (Tasmania) and the Australian mainland. *Battle of St. Vincent* *Spithead and Nore Mutinies* *Battle of Camperdown*
1798	31 January - promoted lieutenant February - journeys to Furneaux Islands off the north-east corner of Van Diemen's Land and notes evidence to support Bass's suspicions about a strait. October - with Bass begins voyage in the *Norfolk* through suspected strait and around Van Diemen's Land. *Battle of the Nile*
1799	January - returns to Port Jackson in the *Norfolk*. Later in year explores northern coast of NSW in the *Norfolk* *Napoleon appointed 1st Consul in France* *French capture Naples*

1800	August - arrives back in England in the *Reliance*.

1800   August - arrives back in England in the *Reliance*.
September - writes to Sir Joseph Banks proposing voyage of discovery to Terra Australis

1801   24 January - appointed to command the sloop *Investigator* on a voyage of Australian exploration
16 February - promoted to rank of commander
17 April - marries Ann Chappelle
18 July - sails for Australia
December - reaches Cape Leeuwin, south-western Australia
Battle of Copenhagen
Armistice with France
End of Pitt the Younger as PM

1802   January - begins survey of southern coast of Australia
April - meets with Baudin in French exploration ship *Géographe* at Encounter Bay, off South Australia
May - reaches Port Jackson (Sydney)
July - sails from Port Jackson to commence survey of east and north coast.
Treaty of Amiens with France signed

1803   March - puts into Timor for repairs to the *Investigator*
June - arrives back in Port Jackson via western and southern coasts having circumnavigated Australia
August - departs Port Jackson as passenger in the *Porpoise* to return to England, the *Investigator* having been condemned - *Porpoise* wrecked on Wreck Reef, returns to Port Jackson in the cutter *Hope*
September - sails from Port Jackson in the schooner *Cumberland* to return to England
15 December - puts into Ile de France (Mauritius), arrested as a spy. Held prisoner in the *Hotel Marengo*
England declares War on France
Napoleonic Wars start

1804   April - moved to the Maison Despeaux, the Garden Prison
Spain declares War on England
Wm. Pitt the Younger returns as PM

1805   August - moved to 'le Refuge' at Plaines Wilhelm, home of the d'Arifat family
Battle of Trafalgar

1806	21 March - French government approves his release
	Wm. Pitt the Younger dies

1807   July - news of French government approval for release reaches Mauritius but General Decaen refuses to implement

1808   *Peninsular War to drive French out of Spain*

1810   13 June - released from Mauritius to return to England via Cape of Good Hope in the *Otter*.
23 October - arrives back in England after absence of over nine years, is promoted Post Captain back dated to 7 May 1810.
December - Mauritius falls to Britain

1812   1 April - birth of only child, Anne
War with America
Napoleon invades Russia, is forced to retreat from Moscow

1814   18 July - *A Voyage to Terra Australis* is published; Died of kidney failure next day - buried St James', Hampstead Road, London
Napoleon abdicates, exiled on Elba

1815   *Waterloo - Napoleonic Wars end, Napoleon imprisoned on island of St. Helena.*

Sources: Baker, Sidney J., *My Own Destroyer: A Biography of Matthew Flinders, Explorer and Navigator*, (Sydney, Currawong, 1962);
Hibbert, Christopher, *Nelson: a Personal History*, (London, Penguin Group, 1994);
Pineo, Huguette, Ly-Tio-Fane, *In the Grips of the Eagle: Matthew Flinders at Ile de France, 1803-1810*, (Mauritius, Mahatma Gandhi Institute, 1988);
Thomas, Sarah, *The Encounter 1802: Art of the Flinders & Baudin Voyages*, (Adelaide, Art Gallery of South Australia, 2002);
Tiley, Robert, *Australian Navigators*, (Sydney, Kangaroo Press, 2002).

Appendix B - Matthew Flinders' Ships

SHIP'S NAME	RATE	GUNS	DATE FROM	DATE TO	TIME (yrs/mths/days)	Posn./Rank
ALERT	Sloop	14	23 Oct 1789	16 May 1790	6m 24 d	Lieut.'s Servant (did not join)
SCIPIO	3rd Rate	64	17 May 1790	27 July 1790	2m 12d	Able Seaman
BELLEROPHON	3rd Rate	74	28 July 1790	30 July 1790	3d	Able Seaman
			31 July 1790	13 April 1791	8m 14d	Midshipman
DICTATOR	3rd Rate	64	14 April 1791	7 May 1791	25d	Midshipman
PROVIDENCE	Sloop	12	8 May 1791	1 April 1793	1yr 10m 25d	Midshipman
			2 April 1793	6 September 1793	5m 25d	Able Seaman
BELLEROPHON	3rd Rate	74	7 September 1793	30 September 1793	24d	Able Seaman
			1 October 1793	10 August 1794	10m 10d	Midshipman
RELIANCE	Discovery Vessel	20	11 August 1794	24 November 1795	1yr 3m 15d	Master's Mate
			25 November 1795	21 January 1797	1yr 1m 28d	Act. Lieut.
TOM THUMB	Cutter		1795			
TOM THUMB II	Cutter		1796			
NORFOLK	Sloop		1798			
FRANCIS	Schooner 5		1798			
NORFOLK	Sloop	31 January	1799			promoted Lieutenant
RELIANCE	Discovery Vessel	20		1800		

SHIP'S NAME	RATE	GUNS	DATE FROM	DATE TO	TIME (yrs/mths/days)	Posn./Rank
INVESTIGATOR	Sloop	22	24 January 1801	15 February 1801	22 d	Lieutenant
			16 February 1801	9 August 1803	2yr 5m 24d	Commander
PORPOISE	Armed Vessel	10	10 August 1803	17 August 1803	8d	Commander (not in command)
HOPE	Cutter	Nil	18 August 1803	8 September 1803	21d	Commander
CUMBERLAND	Schooner	Nil	21 September 1803	18 December 1803	2m 27d	Commander
RAMILLIES	3rd Rate	74	7 May 1810			promoted post-Captain (did not join)

74

Sources: National Maritime Museum, Greenwich, London: Manuscript: MS. 60/017, FLI/5 - Flinders' Service papers; Colledge J. J., revised by Warlow, Lt-Cdr Ben, *Ships of the Royal Navy*; (London, Greenhill Books, 2003); Mack, James D., *Matthew Flinders: 1774-1814*, (Melbourne, Nelson, 1966)

Appendix C:
Key Figures in Matthew Flinders Life

Madame Louise Geneviève La Bauve d'Arifat (née de Ribes) was born on Ile de France in 1758, the daughter of the island's 'procureur-général' and a member of the Conseil Supérieur. Married, 18 November 1777, Marc Antoine de la Bauve d'Arifat, an officer in the Ile de France regiment. They had eight children before she was widowed in 1799. Flinders' hostess at 'Le Refuge', Wilhelms Plaines. Her eldest daughter, Delphine, became close friends with Matthew before her marriage. Madame d'Arifat died on the estate of one of her sons at Black River in the south of the island 10 August 1812.
Sources: Pineo, Huguette, Ly-Tio-Fane, *In the Grips of the Eagle: Matthew Flinders at Ile de France, 1803-1810*, (Mauritius, Mahatma Gandhi Institute, 1988), p.115; Carter, Marina, *Companions of Misfortune: Flinders and Friends at the Isle of France, 1803-1810*, (London, Pink Pigeon Press, 2003), p.178

Sir Joseph Banks was born in London in 1744 and educated at Harrow, Eton and Christ Church, Oxford. In 1766 he made a voyage to Newfoundland collecting plants. Between 1768 and 1771 he accompanied Captain James Cook in his first expedition to the Pacific Ocean and around the world in the *Endeavour*, equipped at his own expense. After leading an expedition to Iceland he was elected President of the Royal Society in 1778, an office he held for forty-one years. His significance lay in his far-reaching influence, rather than through any single personal contribution to science. He founded the African Association, and the colony of New South Wales owed its origin mainly to him through his sponsorship of voyages of discovery. Through him the breadfruit was transferred from Tahiti to the Caribbean, using his life-long friend William Bligh, and he sponsored and equipped Matthew Flinders' voyage to Terra Australis in 1801. Created a baronet in 1781, his name is commemorated in the genus 'Banksia'. He died in 1820.
Source: Parry, Melanie, ed., *Chambers Biographical Dictionary*, (Edinburgh, Chambers Harrap, 1997), p.130

George Bass was born at Aswarby, Lincolnshire in 1771. After training as a physician he joined the Royal Navy and served with Flinders in the *Reliance* between 1795 and 1800. During this period he and Flinders explored the strait between Tasmania and Australia that bears his name, was the first to circumnavigate Tasmania and large parts of the New South Wales coastline and rivers in the *Tom Thumb*. Returning to England in 1800 he set up in business and sailed for Port Jackson with a cargo of merchandise, expecting a good profit from his investment. The venture failed and he tried his luck in the profitable, but dangerous, contraband trade with South America. He sailed for Chile in the *Venus* in 1803 and disappeared without trace.

Sources: Parry, Melanie, ed., *Chambers Biographical Dictionary*, (Edinburgh, Chambers Harrap, 1997), p.147; Brown, Anthony J., *Ill-Starred Captains: Flinders and Baudin*, (London, Chatham Publishing, 2001), p.58

Nicolas Baudin was born at St. Martin on the Ile-de-Ré near La Rochelle on 17 February 1754, the fifth child of merchant parents. Aged fifteen he went to sea as a cabin boy in coastal vessels and in 1774 enlisted in the French Navy as a cadet. In 1775 he went as quartermaster in a troop transport to India. He returned home in 1777 and, commissioned, served in the Caribbean 1779-1780 before commanding the sloop *Apollon* in the English Channel. Relieved of command, he resigned and joined the merchant service. In 1785 he was in command of the *Caroline* carrying emigrants to New Orleans and in 1787 arrived at Port Louis in command of the *Pepita*. From 1787 to 1794 he made four successive voyages on botanical expeditions for the Austrians in *la Jardinière*. Returning to Paris in 1795, he was re-instated and sent to retrieve botanical specimens stored in Trinidad in *la Belle Angélique*. Following the success of this mission he was promoted post-captain and appointed in command of the expedition to Terra Australis in *le Géographe* accompanied by *le Naturaliste*. He sailed from Le Havre on 18 October 1800. After calls into the Ile de France, March-April 1801 and Timor, November 1801, he met Flinders in Encounter Bay, off South Australia, in April 1802. From June-November 1802 his ships lay in Port Jackson, when he again met with Flinders, before returning via Timor to the Ile de France on 7 August 1803, a very sick man. He died there on 16 September 1803.

Sources: Pineo, Huguette, Ly-Tio-Fane, *In the Grips of the Eagle: Matthew Flinders at Ile de France, 1803-1810*, (Mauritius, Mahatma Gandhi Institute, 1988), p.36; Brown, Anthony J., *Ill-Starred Captains: Flinders and Baudin*, (London, Chatham Publishing, 2001), p.21

William Bligh was born at Tinten Manor, St. Tudy, near Plymouth, on 9 September 1754 the only son of an excise officer based in Plymouth. He first went to sea in 1762, aged seven, as a captain's personal servant in the *Monmouth*. He joined the Royal Navy in 1770 and served in HMS *Hunter* before being made up to midshipman in 1771, serving in HMS *Crescent* and HMS *Ranger*. In 1776, aged twenty-two, he sailed with James Cook, as Master of the *Resolution*, on his third and final voyage. He saw action at the battle of Dogger Bank in August 1781 and at Gibraltar in 1782 under Lord Howe. Promoted to Lieutenant 5 October 1781, he married Elizabeth Betham, daughter of a customs officer, the following year, in the Isle of Man; they had six daughters. In 1787 he was chosen by Sir Joseph Banks to command the *Bounty* to transport breadfruit plants from Tahiti to the West Indies. On 28 April 1789 Fletcher Christian led a mutiny and Bligh, with eighteen men, was cast adrift in an open boat which he sailed to Timor,.without charts a journey of 3,618 nautical miles, which took forty-seven days. On his return to England, by court martial, he was exonerated of all blame for the loss of his ship, promoted post-captain 15 December 1790, and given command of the *Falcon*. In 1791 he was given command of the second breadfruit expedition in the *Providence*, where Flinders was a midshipman. In 1797, following directly after the Nore mutiny, he commanded HMS *Director* at the battle of Camperdown and in 1801, in command of HMS *Glatton*, distinguished himself at the battle of Copenhagen for which he was personally commended by Admiral Nelson. The same year he was elected a Fellow of the Royal Society for his services to navigation, hydrography and botany. In 1805 he was appointed Governor of New South Wales but was removed by mutinous soldiers in 1808 during the 'rum-rebellion' inspired by John MacArthur. He was again exonerated of all blame on his return to England in 1810 and promoted Rear-Admiral of the Blue 31 July 1810, Rear-Admiral of the White 12 August 1812, Rear-Admiral of the Red 4 December 1813 and Vice-Admiral of the Blue 4 June 1814. He died in London on 7 December 1817, aged 64.

Sources: Parry, Melanie, ed., *Chambers Biographical Dictionary*, (Edinburgh, Chambers Harrap, 1997), p.215; Syrett, David and Dinardo R.L., *The Commissioned Sea Officers of the Royal Navy 1660-1815*, (Aldershot, Scolar Press for Navy Records Society, 1994), p.38.

Ann Flinders (née Chappelle) was born at Hull, in Lincolnshire on 21 November 1772 the only child of John and Anne Chappelle (née Mallinson). Her father, a sea-captain, died at sea when she was only four. Her mother remarried in 1786 and gave birth to a daughter, Isabella, later that year. The two half-sisters were constant companions from the outset and remained good friends throughout their lives. At the age of twelve she contracted smallpox and as a result was left partially blind in one eye. It is unclear when she first met Matthew except it must have been before he left England in the Reliance in February 1795, which is when their letters begin. They would have met through the sisters of John Franklin who were related to Flinders step-mother. Married in April 1801, three

months before Flinders sailed in the Investigator, his enforced absence for nine years injured her health and nerves. Her only child, Anne, was born 1 April 1812, two years prior to Matthew's death. She died 10 February 1852, aged 79.
Source: Retter, Catherine & Sinclair, Shirley, *Letters to Ann: The Love Story of Matthew Flinders and Ann Chappelle*, (Sydney, HarperCollins, 2001), p.149

Charles Mathieu Isidore Decaen was born at Caen on 13 April 1769. He initially joined the French navy and served in the marine artillery from 1787-1790 before leaving to study law. In 1792 he re-enlisted on outbreak of war, served with distinction under Kléber, promoted captain, fought in Vendée against royalist rebels who he pursued relentlessly after they turned to guerrilla warfare following their defeat at Nantes. Promoted to 'général de brigade' in the Rhine army in 1795; took part in battle of Hohenlinden, under Moreau, against Austrians in 1800. Napoleon personally appointed him Captain-General of French territories east of Cape of Good Hope in 1803, aged thirty-four. After being rebuffed by the British at Pondicherry, when attempting to re-possess the French territories in India, he retreated to the Ile de France on 16 August where he was Governor during Flinders' incarceration there and remained until the British invasion in 1810. On his return to France he was cleared by the Enquiry Commission and given command of the French army of 30,000 men in Catalonia in 1811, and in 1813, was transferred to the Netherlands. In 1814 was appointed to command the 'Gironde Corps' to retake Bordeaux from Wellington. Following the restoration of the monarchy, was given a divisional command by Louis XVIII but rallied to Napoleon on his escape from Elba and Louis XVIII's flight to Ghent. In 1815, after defeat of Napoleon, was imprisoned for fifteen months at Abbaye, during which time his health suffered and he lost his fortune, before being granted an amnesty. He lived in his country house at Cernay in Montmorency as a reserve general until he died in Paris on 9 September 1832. His private thoughts on the Flinders affair were lost to posterity when his private papers were destroyed during the war of 1870-71.
Sources: Pineo, Huguette, Ly-Tio-Fane, *In the Grips of the Eagle: Matthew Flinders at Ile de France, 1803-1810*, (Mauritius, Mahatma Gandhi Institute, 1988), pp.43, 169; Brown, Anthony J., *Ill-Starred Captains: Flinders and Baudin*, (London, Chatham Publishing, 2001), p.491

Dr Mathew Flinders was born at Donington-in-Holland, in Lincolnshire on 17 February 1750, the youngest son of Dr John and Elizabeth (née Hursthouse) Flinders, and father of Matthew Flinders. A surgeon-apothecary he married twice, firstly Susannah Ward, Matthew's mother in 1773 and, after her death on 23 March 1783, Elizabeth Ellis (née Weekes) on 2 December 1783. He fathered nine children by his first wife. Matthew was the second and eldest son, of whom five survived beyond infancy, and two by his second wife. As the eldest son Matthew was expected to follow his father in the family business and the rift caused when he went to sea was never fully healed. He died on 1 May 1802.

Source: Cawthen, John, Dr Mathew Flinders' Diaries, (unpublished transcript of extracts from two original diaries held in Lincolnshire Archives, January 2002)

Samuel Ward Flinders was born at Donington, Lincolnshire in November 1782, younger brother of Matthew Flinders. Enlisted in Royal Navy as a volunteer in HMS *Reliance* 1784 (age twelve) to accompany Matthew (senior master's mate, later second lieutenant) on voyage to New South Wales. Returned to England 1800, promoted lieutenant March 1801 and appointed to the *Investigator* at Matthew's request. After being shipwrecked in the *Porpoise* returned to England in the East Indiaman *Earl Camden* under Nathaniel Dance. Awarded ceremonial sword for his part in action against French squadron under Linois off Pulo Auro. Served in Channel Fleet, appointed to command of gun-brig *Bloodhound* 12 in 1806; court-martialled for disobedience of orders 1808, dismissed ship and docked three years' seniority. Subsequently retired on half-pay. Died 1834, buried at Donington.

Source: Brown, Anthony J., *Ill-Starred Captains: Flinders and Baudin*, (London, Chatham Publishing, 2001), p.492

Robert Merrick Fowler was born at Horncastle, Lincolnshire in 1778 and entered the Royal Navy as a volunteer in May 1793. Served as midshipman in the *Royal William* 100, *Hector* 74, *Cumberland* 74, and *Royal George* 100, flagship of Admiral Lord Bridport. Promoted lieutenant February 1800, joined the *Xenophon*, under command of John Henry Martin, (later *Investigator*) as first lieutenant; Flinders' second-in-command 1801-1803. Appointed to command the *Porpoise* taking Flinders back to England, wrecked August 1803; exonerated by court martial at Portsmouth of responsibility for shipwreck in 1804. Returned to England via Canton as passenger in East Indiaman, *Earl Camden*, Captain Nathaniel Dance. Assisted Dance in driving off French squadron under Admiral Linois at Pulo Auro in February 1804. Subsequently promoted commander in 1806, saw active service in home and Caribbean waters, 1806-1811. Promoted post-captain 1811, placed on half-pay 1812, promoted Rear-Admiral 1846.

Sources: Brown, Anthony J., *Ill-Starred Captains: Flinders and Baudin*, (London, Chatham Publishing, 2001), p.492; O'Byrne, William R., *A Naval Biographical Dictionary*, (2 Vols., Polstead, Suffolk, J B Hayward and Son, 1990), p.375

John Hunter was born in Leith in 1737 and studied for the ministry at Aberdeen University but left at age seventeen to join the Royal Navy. In 1786 he was appointed second captain of the *Sirius*, flagship of the first fleet, which was to sail to Australia under the command of Captain Arthur Phillip. He returned to England in 1792 after circumnavigating the globe and being shipwrecked on Norfolk Island. In 1795 he returned to New South Wales in the *Reliance*, where he met Flinders, as its second governor. During his governorship he encouraged the exploratory voyages of George Bass and Matthew Flinders, and as a keen natural scientist he promoted many valuable expeditions in search of botanical and zoological specimens. However, he made many powerful enemies due to the clash between the military and civil government in New South Wales and was recalled to London in 1800. He died in 1821.
Source: Parry, Melanie, ed., *Chambers Biographical Dictionary*, (Edinburgh, Chambers Harrap, 1997), p.939

Philip Gidley King was born at Launceston, Cornwall, in April 1758 and joined the Royal Navy as a captain's servant in December 1770. He served in the East Indies from 1771-1775 and in American waters from 1775-1778 before being promoted Lieutenant in 1780. Served under Captain Arthur Phillip 1782-1783. Accompanied Phillip, first governor of New South Wales, as second lieutenant in HMS *Sirius*, flagship of First Fleet; established settlement on Norfolk Island, February 1788. Lieutenant governor of Norfolk Island 1791-1796; promoted post-captain 1798, and appointed third governor of New South Wales 1800. He encouraged exploration, increased colony's trading links, and sought to control trafficking in liquor; in 1803 he established first settlement in Van Diemen's Land. Failing health and opposition to his policies in London induced him to offer his resignation in 1803, but he was not replaced until 1806, by Governor Bligh. Returned to England 1807, died in London, September 1808.
Source: Brown, Anthony J., *Ill-Starred Captains: Flinders and Baudin*, (London, Chatham Publishing, 2001), p.494

Sir Thomas Pasley was born on 2 March 1734 and after joining the Royal Navy, served as a midshipman under Captains Willett, Cockburn and Webber. Promoted to acting-lieutenant, he sailed under Captain Digby on the unfortunate expedition against Rochefort but was confirmed in the rank on returning to England. He then served in the fireship *Roman Emperor* and the frigates *Hussar* and *Aeolus*. In the *Aeolus* he distinguished himself in the capture of *La Mignonne* 20, on 19 March 1759, and the next year on 28 February 1760, when in company with the *Brilliant* and the *Pallas* 36, the

French frigates *Belleisle, Blonde* and *Terpischore* were taken. After leaving the *Aeolus* in 1762 he was promoted to Commander and given command first of the sloop *Albany,* and then the sloop *Weasel,* before being promoted to post-captain in 1771. He then served in the *Seahorse* 20, *Glasgow, Sibylle* 28, *Jupiter* 50 and *Bellerophon* 74. He was present, in the *Jupiter* in 1781, at the encounter between Commodore Johnstone and M. de Suffrein in Port Playa Bay. From 1788 until 1793 he was in command, in the rank of Commodore, of all ships lying in the Medway. In 1793 he returned to command the *Bellerophon* where he continued to fly his flag under Lord Howe when promoted to Rear-Admiral in April 1794. Under his command the ship played a vital role at the 'Battle of the Glorious First of June' but he lost a leg in the action. Then created a Baronet and awarded a pension of '1,000 shillings per year' he was promoted Vice-Admiral on 1 June 1795. In 1798 he went as Commander-in-Chief of the Medway and in 1799 to Plymouth as Port Admiral. He died, Admiral-of-the-White on 29 November 1808.
Source: O'Byrne, William R., *A Naval Biographical Dictionary*, (2 Vols., Polstead, Suffolk, J B Hayward and Son, 1990), p.870

Charles Thomi Pitot was born on 8 November 1779 on Ile de France, his family belonged to the old nobility established on the island. Taken by his parents to Paris in 1782 he, and his brother Edouard, studied there following the death of their father and until the setting up of the National Assembly. Under the revolutionary government the brothers lost all their money and in 1790 were imprisoned. Fortuitously liberated they returned to Ile de France in 1793 and set up in business. As secretary of the Society of Science and Art of Ile de France he became Flinders' closest friend on the island and wrote many letters to influential persons in Paris pleading for the navigator's early release. Following the British invasion he became the *de facto* leader of the French Mauritians under Governor Farquhar. He died 23 May 1821 and is buried on the island at Pamplemousses.
Sources: Pineo, Huguette, Ly-Tio-Fane, *In the Grips of the Eagle: Matthew Flinders at Ile de France, 1803-1810*, (Mauritius, Mahatma Gandhi Institute, 1988), p.96; Carter, Marina, *Companions of Misfortune: Flinders and Friends at the Isle of France, 1803-1810*, (London, Pink Pigeon Press, 2003), p.183

Bibliography

A. MANUSCRIPT SOURCES:

BRITISH LIBRARY, LONDON

Manuscripts: MSS. 8100. 32,439, Letters from Flinders to Sir Joseph Banks 1801-1812

CARNEGIE LIBRARY, CUREPIPE, MAURITIUS

1806-1813, Letters from Flinders to Charles Thomy Pitot

LINCOLNSHIRE COUNTY ARCHIVES, LINCOLN

Flinders Senior, Mathew, Diary and Account Book, 1775-1803

MITCHELL LIBRARY, STATE LIBRARY of NEW SOUTH WALES

Flinders, Matthew, Private Diary (Journal), December 17 1803-July 4 1814

Flinders, Matthew, Private Letter Books, 27 November 1801-23 May 1814, 3 Vols. (A79-4/5)

Sir Joseph Banks' Papers, Section 13, Series 65; Letters received by Banks from Flinders between 6 September 1800-13 December 1811.

Sir Joseph Banks' Papers - Brabourne Collection, Vol.7, King 1788-1805, (A78-6); King to Banks, 21 July 1805, King's efforts to obtain release of Flinders from Ile de France; his condemnation of Investigator upheld, pp.265-6; Vol.16, Misc. Correspondence, p.167; 20 September 1806, order for liberation of Flinders received by Banks, sent from France two months earlier; 5 May 1809, order for liberation of Flinders, signed by Napoleon, forwarded by Banks and delivered under flag of truce to Decaen; Vols. 11-12 (A79-4/5), Letters re-Flinders' imprisonment, 1804-1808. King Papers, Vol.8 and Further Papers; Letter Banks to King, 29 August 1804, p.118a; Banks to King, 20 September 1806, order for release of Flinders, to be exchanged for Capt. Milius, p.210.

NATIONAL MARITIME MUSEUM, GREENWICH, LONDON

Adm/L/Y/55 - *Investigator* Log (This only has the short period 26 January 1801 - 8 March 1801 written by Lt. Robert Fowler, 1st Lieutenant)

Manuscript: MS. 60/017
FLI/1 - Letters: Banks to Flinders and his wife, 1800-14

FLI/2 - Letters: From French friends on Mauritius to Flinders 1804-15.
FLI/3 - Letters: Official papers received by Flinders 1801-12.
FLI/4 - Letters: Copies of letters written by Flinders 1795-1808.
FLI/5 - Flinders' Service papers.
FLI/8a - Portion of Journal, relating to voyage in *Providence* with Bligh, c.1791.
FLI/25 - Letters written by Flinders to his wife, 1799-1812
Reg. No. 6224, Box 661, HMS *Investigator* Deck Plans, Sheerness Yard, 1801

PUBLIC RECORD OFFICE, KEW, LONDON

Adm.1 - Papers (correspondence): Admirals' Despatches, Captains, Lieutenants, Hydrographic Office, Reports
/4187, 1802, Lady Nelson placed under Flinders' command
/4197, 4 September 1804, Flinders' account of his detention at Ile de France
Adm.2 - Secretary's Dept., Out-letters
/293/484, Navy Board Letter of 21 November 1800
Adm.7 - Admiralty Secretary, Miscellanea
/707,708 - Flinders' Narrative of Imprisonment by French, 1806
Adm.13/102 - Courts Martial
Adm. 37, 38, 39, 41, 115 & 119 - Ships' Musters (*Providence*)
Adm. 35/1361 - Pay Books (*Providence*)
Adm.51 - Captains Logs
/4551, 4552 - *Providence* (1792-93) - Bligh
Adm.55 - Ships' Logs (exploration) /75, 76 - *Investigator*
/78 - *Cumberland*
/97, 98 - *Providence* (Flinders Log)
/152, 153 - *Providence* (Bligh)
Adm.95 -
/7, Deptford Yard Estimates for building ships 1795-1797
/23-62, Ships' Sailing Qualities
Adm.101 - Surgeons' Logs
Adm.106 - Navy Board Records
/2508, Navy Board Standing Orders
/3323, Deptford Yard Book dated 1791
/3368, Deptford Yard Book, second series
/3412, Deptford Yard Book dated 17.4. 1798
/3472, Deptford Yard Letter Book dated 5.4.1782
/3555, Sheerness Yard Letters, 1798-1799
/3556, Sheerness Yard Letters, 1800-1801
Adm.110 - Victualling Board, Out-Letters
Adm.180 - /9, Progress Books
/23, Dimension Book

STATE LIBRARY of VICTORIA, MELBOURNE

La Trobe Collections, Flinders' Papers, Manuscript Collection, 546/7

B. PRIMARY PRINTED SOURCES:

Bligh, Captain William, *The Log of the Providence1791-1793*, (Guildford, Genesis Publications, 1976)

Flinders, Matthew, *A Voyage to Terra Australis*, (2 Vols. atlas, London, G & W Nicol, 1814)

Flinders, Matthew, letters, *Historical Records of New South Wales*, Vol. V, 1803-1805

C. MAGAZINES and NEWSPAPERS:

FLINDERS UNIVERSITY of SOUTH AUSTRALIA:
Central Library Special Collections: Items from Flinders' Collection

EPH 9502: Purdon, N., 'Matthew Flinders: the investigator of himself', *The Adelaide Review*, January 1987, pp.10-11

EPH 9512: Farwell, G., 'More Light on Flinders, (review of Mack, J., *Matthew Flinders, 1774-1814*)', Sydney Morning Herald, 1 October 1966, p.17

EPH 7060: 'Ellis, M.H., Psycho-analysing Matthew Flinders, (review of Baker, S.J., *My Own Destroyer*)', The Bulletin, 13 October 1962, pp.38-39

EPH 7065: May W.E., 'The man who named Australia', *The Geographical Magazine (National Geographic)*, Vol. 21(8), December 1948, pp.306-311

D. SECONDARY PRINTED SOURCES:
N.B. The place of publication, unless otherwise stated, is London.

Austin, K.A., *The Voyage of the Investigator: Commander Matthew Flinders RN*, (Adelaide, Rigby (Seal Books) 1968 (1964))

Baker, Sidney J., *My Own Destroyer: A Biography of Matthew Flinders, Explorer and Navigator*, (Sydney, Currawong, 1962)

Brown, Anthony J., *Ill-Starred Captains: Flinders and Baudin*, (Chatham Publishing, 2001)

Bryant, Joseph., *Captain Matthew Flinders, R.N. His Voyages, Discoveries and Fortunes,* (1928)

Carter, Marina, *Companions of Misfortune: Flinders and Friends at the Isle of France, 1803-1810*, (Pink Pigeon Press, 2003)

Chittleborough, Anne; Dooley, Gillian; Glover, Brenda & Hosking, Rick, *Alas, for the Pelicans! Flinders, Baudin & Beyond: Essays & Poems*, (South Australia, Wakefield Press 2002)

Colledge J. J., revised by Warlow, Lt-Cdr Ben, *Ships of the Royal Navy*, (Greenhill Books, 2003)

Estensen, Miriam, *The Life of Matthew Flinders*, (Crows Nest NSW 2065, Allen & Unwin, 2003)

Flannery, Tim, ed. & intro., *Terra Australis:Matthew Flinders' Great Adventures in the Circumnavigation of Australia*, (Melbourne, Text Publishing, 2000)

Gertsakis, Elizabeth, *The Lost Letters of Ann Chappelle Flinders*, (Adelaide, Flinders University, 2002)

Hill, Ernestine, *My Love Must Wait-The Story of Matthew Flinders*, (Sydney, Angus and Robertson, 1955)

Ingleton, Geoffrey C., *Matthew Flinders, Navigator and Chartmaker*, (Guildford, Genesis Publications, 1986)

Ly-Tio-Fane, *Madeleine, Le Géographe et le Naturaliste à L'Île de France 1801,1803: Ultime Escale du Capitaine Baudin*, (Port Louis, Les Auteurs, 2003)

Mack, James D., *Matthew Flinders: 1774-1814*, (Melbourne, Nelson, 1966)

Monteath, Peter, ed. & intro., *Sailing with Flinders: The Journal of Seaman Samuel Smith*, (Adelaide, Corkwood Press, 2002)

O'Byrne, William R., *A Naval Biographical Dictionary*, (2 Vols., Polstead, Suffolk, J B Hayward and Son, 1990)

Parry, Melanie, ed., *Chambers Biographical Dictionary*, (Edinburgh, Chambers Harrap, 1997)

Peron, Francois, trans. Philips, Richard, *A Voyage to the Southern Hemisphere*, 1809, (reprinted, Melbourne, Marsh Walsh Publishing, 1975)

Pineo, Huguette, Ly-Tio-Fane, *In the Grips of the Eagle: Matthew Flinders at Ile de France, 1803-1810*, (Mauritius, Mahatma Gandhi Institute, 1988)

Retter, Catherine & Sinclair, Shirley, *Letters to Ann: The Love Story of Matthew Flinders and Ann Chappelle*, (Sydney, HarperCollins, 2001)

Ritchie G.S., *The Admiralty Chart*, (Hollis and Carter, 1967)

Russell, R. W., *Matthew Flinders-The Ifs of History*, (Adelaide, Flinders University, 1979)

Scott, Ernest, *The Life of Matthew Flinders*, (Sydney, Harper Collins, 2001 (1914))

Syrett, David and Dinardo R.L., *The Commissioned Sea Officers of the Royal Navy 1660-1815*, (Aldershot, Scolar Press for Navy Records Society, 1994)

Thomas, Sarah, The Encounter 1802: *Art of the Flinders & Baudin Voyages,* ,(Adelaide, Art Gallery of South Australia, 2002)

Tiley, Robert, *Australian Navigators*, (Sydney, Kangaroo Press, 2002)

E. JOURNAL ARTICLES:

FLINDERS UNIVERSITY of SOUTH AUSTRALIA:
Central Library Special Collections: Items from Flinders Collection

EPH 7002: 'Biographical Memoir of Matthew Flinders, R.N.', *Naval Chronicle*, Vol.32, (1814), pp.177-191

EPH 7051: McCrae, G.G., 'Geographical discoveries and explorers of the 18th century and earlier part of the 19th century - La Perouse and Baudin in New South Wales, and Flinders in Mauritius: their experience at the hands of colonial officials', *Royal Geographic Society*, Victoria, Vol.29, (1912), pp.1-19

EPH 7021: Mault, A., 'Detention of Flinders at Mauritius', *Royal Society of Tasmania*, Paper 18, (1889), pp.121-124

EPH 7023: General Decaen, 'Report on the Detention of Flinders', *Royal Geographic Society of Australasia*, Proceedings Vol.12, (1910-1911), pp.36-41

The Mariner's Mirror

Darby, Madge, 'Bligh's Disciple: Matthew Flinders' Journals of HMS *Providence* (1791-93)', *The Mariner's Mirror*, vol.86, no.4, (2000), pp. 401-411

Geeson, N.T., and Sexton, R.T., 'H.M. Sloop *Investigator*', *The Mariner's Mirror*, vol.56, no.3, (1970), pp. 275-298

May, W.E.,Commander, RN. 'The History of the Magnetic Compass', *The Mariner's Mirror*, vol.38, no.3, (1952), pp. 210-222

F. TYPESCRIPT and UNPUBLISHED STUDIES:

Cawthen, John, 'Dr Mathew Flinders Diaries', (unpublished transcript of extracts from two original diaries held in Lincolnshire Archives, January 2002)

Hitchcock, W, 'Matthew Flinders in Mauritius 1803-1810', (unpublished transcript of Flinders Journal of his time at Mauritius, December 2003)

Milazzo, Stephen, AO FRACP, Flinders' Last Illness: The Final Five Months of the Journal, February-July 1814: A Medical Interpretation (forthcoming)